MARITIME HERITAGE

Barrow & Morecambe Bay

Raymond Sankey

Silver Link Publishing Ltd

The Trundle, Ringstead Road,
Great Addington, Kettering,
Northants NN14 4BW

First published in the United Kingdom, August 1986.
Reprinted November 1991

ISBN 0 947971 07 6

Designed by Nigel Harris.
Front Cover design by Phil Cousins

Typeset by Dentset, Oxford and printed in the United Kingdom by Woolnough Bookbinding Limited, Irthlingborough, Northamptonshire.

Sankey, Raymond
Maritime heritage : Barrow & Morecambe Bay.
1. Shipping——Morecambe Bay——History
——20th century. 2. Morecambe Bay (England)——
History
I. Title
623.8'2'00942769 HE826

ISBN 0–947971–07–6

CONTENTS

ACKNOWLEDGEMENTS

I MUST place on record my sincere thanks and appreciation to all those people who have, in various ways, given me their help in gathering together the material for this book. I would firstly thank the press officers of Vickers Shipbuilding & Engineering Ltd, for supplying a complete list of ships built at the Barrow yard, together with launching dates and other details: this information made the task of caption writing much easier.

Thanks are also due to David Hughes, of Barrow Museum, for much assistance given in compiling this book, also to K.E. Royall and Fred Strike, of Barrow. Also many thanks indeed to my friend Ken J. Norman, of Barrow, for his assistance with research.

FRONT COVER: The Peninsular & Orient Steam Navigation Company liner *Strathallan* leaves the fitting-out berth in Buccleuch Dock, at Vickers yard, following completion in March 1938. This ship was torpedoed and subsequently sunk in December 1942.

PREVIOUS PAGE: The Isle of Man Steam Packet Company's *Ben-My-Chree*, completed in 1927 and the fourth of the Company's vessels to carry this historic Manx name. The ship is painted in the white livery applied to the Manx fleet after 1932: the traditional black livery with white superstructure returned after World War II.

LEFT: The Brazilian Navy's *Sao Paulo* (left) lies alongside the Royal Navy's 'St Vincent' class battleship *HMS Vanguard* (completed March 1 1910) in Buccleuch Dock, Barrow.

BACK COVER: Above: 'M' class submarine monitor No. M2 in original condition, fitted with one 12in. gun and a single 3in. anti-aircraft gun. The 12in. weapon was subsequently removed and replaced with a small aircraft hangar: Below: Battle Cruiser *HMS Princess Royal* as completed by Vickers in November 1912 for the Royal Navy.

FOREWORD

By
MICHAEL CROWDY
CHAIRMAN, WORLD SHIP SOCIETY

WHEN I first learned that this book was being compiled I wondered precisely what the subject matter would be, but having for many years been an admirer of the work of Raymond Sankey and his father, I was confident that the end product would be full of interest.

I have not been disappointed and I doubt if the reader will be either. Barrow has been the cradle of many fine warships (battleships, cruisers and destroyers) as well as elegant passenger liners of the highest class. The town's shipbuilders have always been in the forefront of technology and this is reflected by this book: one of the most significant pictures in these pages is of Holland No. 2, one of the very earliest submarines in the Royal Navy and a 'forefather' of the RN's nuclear submarines, some of which Vickers have also built.

But there are other 'gems': views of the passenger steamers which sailed from Barrow and Fleetwood; the paddle tug *Walney* carrying rather more passengers than she should have done, and pictures of some of the less-glamorous ships that were built at Barrow. The photographs are well-chosen and they repay careful attention for the detail they reveal.

There is much to interest the ship enthusiast in this book, but local people and visitors to the area will also find much of appeal. Those who have sailed aboard the *MV Teal* on Windermere and wondered how she arrived there will find their questions answered by the picture of her prefabricated hull loaded on a train at Barrow Docks, awaiting delivery to Lakeside where she was rebuilt on the slipway. The photographs are indeed fascinating and this book will hold the interest of the marine historian and the ship modeller alike.

Silver Link Publishing is already well-known in the realm of railway publishing and I hope that success with this book will encourage the company to expand further into the equally fascinating area of shipping publishing.

In June 1950, the newly-completed Peninsular & Orient Steam Navigation Company's liner *Chusan* is turned in Ramsden Dock, Barrow, by the tugs *Dongarth* and *Yorkgarth*, prior to being towed stern-first into Walney Channel. Launched on June 28 1949 by Viscountess Bruce, *Chusan* was 24,261 tons (gross) and 672.5ft. long with a beam of 85.2ft. and a draught of 29ft. Her six geared steam turbines, built by Vickers, were rated at 42,500 shaft horsepower and drove twin shafts giving *Chusan* a speed of 22 knots. She carried 464 first class and 541 tourist class passengers and she was the earliest large ship to be fitted with Denny Brown stabilisers as part of her original equipment: *Chusan* immediately eclipsed her running mates on P&O's Far East service, but after 1959 she was used extensively on round-the-world cruises and trans-Pacific voyages. She was withdrawn in 1973.

INTRODUCTION

A proud moment: on April 5 1939 shipyard workers on the slipway are dwarfed by the towering hull of the aircraft carrier *HMS Illustrious* as she glides into the Walney Channel, just less than two years after being laid down, on April 27 1937. This ship had a displacement of 23,000 tons, with an overall length of 753½ft. and a beam of nearly 96ft. Driven by geared steam turbines of 110,000SHP, its triple screws gave *HMS Illustrious* a speed of 31 knots, and the ship was completed on May 25 1940, after which she went on to a distinguished war career, chiefly in the Mediterranean.

WHEN my father Edward Sankey started producing photographic postcards in the 1890s the main subjects were views in and around his home town of Barrow in Furness. He gained ground rapidly as a commercial photographer, and in the early years of the 20th century he became an official photographer for the Furness Railway Company.

This broadened his scope considerably and amongst other things, led to him starting to take photographs depicting the regular steamer sailings which plied the waters of Morecambe Bay between Barrow-in-Furness and Fleetwood. The FR operated these services using the elegant paddle steamers *Lady Moyra* and *Lady Evelyn*. It was on these sailings that the maritime section of the Sankey Collection began.

During each summer season hundreds of photographs would be taken aboard the steamers, and the chance to photograph a passing vessel, of whatever size, was rarely missed. I have been asked about how the Sankey Collection came about and the simple answer is that it wasn't planned at all — it just grew from that small beginning on the Barrow-Fleetwood service. The postcard-buying public certainly endorsed my father's choice, for there was always a healthy demand for postcards showing ships sailing in and out of the ports of Morecambe Bay — especially Barrow and Fleetwood.

Of these pre-1914 scenes I had no detailed knowledge and in some cases the details available in our records are a little sketchy. However, there are always good friends who are willing to help and I am grateful for the help I've received in putting this book together. My own recollections of the steamers *Lady Moyra* and *Lady Evelyn* are boyhood memories of these vessels, on which I sailed many times. I always preferred the *Lady Moyra*, for she had two funnels and, in my youthful view at the time, it therefore had to be a better ship! This was not as odd as it might sound however, for in the 1930s it became apparent that this belief was more widespread amongst older members of the population. In 1931 the

Peninsular & Orient Steam Navigation Company ship *Strathnaver* slipped into the Walney Channel and was towed to the fitting-out berth in Buccleuch Dock. There the ship was fitted with three funnels, of which only the centre structure actually carried smoke from the boiler rooms. The fore and aft funnels were 'dummies,' fitted to make the ship more popular with a travelling public which had come to believe that 'real' ships never had only a single funnel! In later years the 'dummies' were removed to create more deck space.

As any photographer will appreciate, ships make marvellous photographic subjects, and launches at Vickers' yard, or the departure of the completed ship, were always good postcard subjects and our output contributed steadily to the growing collection of maritime pictures in our Collection.

I was very familiar with ships from accompanying my father whilst in my school days, but there was a special excitement when I joined the family business in the early 1920s and started taking my own photographs commercially. The first ship launch I photographed was that of the Orient Steam Navigation Company's *Orama*, in May 1924, the first large liner to be launched at the Vickers yard after several years of depression in the shipyard. Photographing launches was not always without incident and mishap however, and one such occasion took place on March 1 1934, when *HMS Ajax* slid down the slipway into the Walney Channel.

At launches a special platform was constructed from which press photographers and newsreel cameramen could get the best view of the ship entering the water. This platform was naturally very close to the action, and as *HMS Ajax* (a 'Leander' class cruiser) began to slide into the water the drag chains (which pulled taut as the ship became afloat to stop it drifting too far) landed heavily on our platform, three times in succession. This was particularly alarming as the platform was 20ft off the ground and the heavy chains threatened to take us and our equipment into the channel with each blow. Fortunately the platform survived and I am pleased to say that I didn't miss the shot! The still photographs of course give no hint of the drama but the newsreel cameramen found it impossible to keep filming through the ordeal and each time the chains hit the platform they retreated very rapidly from their equipment, and then returned to resume filming. Thus, in the completed newsreels *HMS Ajax* makes three quite distinct and disjointed jumps into the sea. I have covered many launches since then but I never came nearer to missing the shot!

Cunard-White Star's *Scythia*, launched by Vickers in March 1920, is manoeuvred by tugs in the docks at Barrow. *Scythia* worked for nearly 40 years: she was scrapped in 1958.

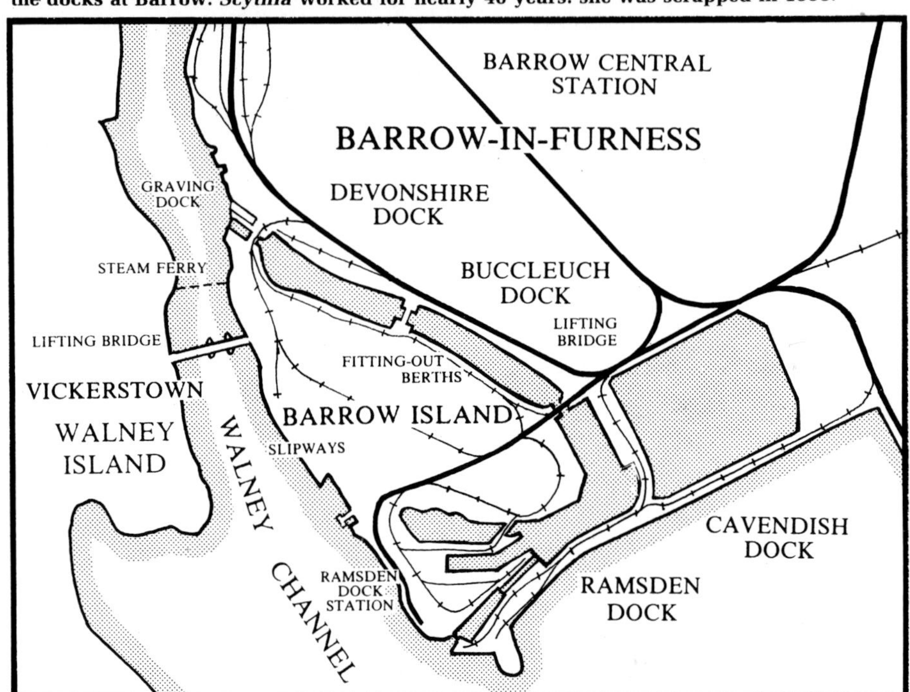

Above: a map of the dock system at Barrow, showing the slipway site, adjacent to the Walney Channel, from where newly launched ships were towed through Ramsden Dock to the fitting-out berths in Devonshire or Buccleuch Docks.

This book is not designed to be a comprehensive pictorial history of Barrow, or Morecambe Bay: it is a selective look at the shipping activity in the area over the 80 or so years that my family's photographic business was at work. They were very interesting years and many favourite ships can be seen in the following pages. The book starts with the Morecambe Bay passenger steamers and goes on to recall warship building and repair at Barrow, submarine construction, the elegant liners of the inter-war years, the less-glamorous cargo ships and freighters which were once so common, and the everyday dock business of Barrow as a port. Within each section I have followed a roughly chronological path through the ships featured. I hope that the photographs I have selected from the Sankey Collection give readers as much pleasure as they have given me in printing them again!

Raymond Sankey,
Ulverston, Cumbria, April 1986.

THE PASSENGER STEAMERS OF MORECAMBE BAY

AT THE TIME the Sankey Collection of photographs was starting to grow, Morecambe Bay was used by a variety of passenger and pleasure steamers. The Furness Railway operated a paddle steamer service between Barrow and Fleetwood, while the Midland and London & North Western Railways, Lancashire & Yorkshire and the Isle of Man Steam Packet Company operated services to the Isle of Man from Fleetwood and Heysham. There were also passenger sailings from Barrow to Belfast and the Isle of Man, operated by the Barrow Steam Navigation Company, together with the activities of a handful of small steamers which gave pleasure sailings in the Bay, from Blackpool or Fleetwood. My father spent much of his time photographing this rich pattern of activity in the Bay, to which this first chapter is devoted.

FURNESS RAILWAY PADDLE STEAMERS

TRADITIONALLY the Furness Railway's income had been derived from the carrying of iron ore, and associated traffic, but as this business declined towards the end of the 19th century, the FR decided to develop its passenger and tourist traffic to a greater extent. In order to gain a share of the potentially lucrative business from the Fylde Coast, the FR decided to start a Fleetwood-Barrow steamer service, with through bookings available from Blackpool. For this service the Company bought the *PS Lady Evelyn*, (above) built by J. Scott, & Co, at Kinghorn in 1900, and the service was so successful that in 1904 it was decided to lengthen her by 30ft. to increase passenger capacity, and this conversion was completed in 1905. The vessel was requisitioned for mine-sweeping in World War I and on her return from military service in 1918 was sold to W.H. Tucker for service in the Bristol Channel. *Lady Evelyn* was later a member of the Campbell south coast's fleet and as the *Brighton Belle* was lost at Dunkirk in May 1940 The vessel was 170ft. long (lengthened to 200ft.) with a beam of 24.1ft. and a depth of 8.2ft. The gross tonnage was 230 and the steamer was driven by twin-cylinder compound engines.

Above, right: The Bristol Channel steamer *Gwalia*, built at Clydebank in 1905, was bought by the FR in 1910 and renamed *Lady Moyra* to give greater capacity on the Barrow-Fleetwood service. *Lady Moyra* could accommodate 1,015 passengers, against *Lady Evelyn's* 714, The newer vessel was also 3 knots faster and on occasion completed the Barrow-Fleetwood run in 45 minutes, though 1¼hr. was judged to be the normal time. She served on the Fleetwood service until September 1914, after which she was requisitioned as a mine-sweeper. After the war she also became part of the Campbell south coast fleet and as the *Brighton Queen* was sunk at Dunkirk. The vessel had a gross tonnage of 807 and was 254ft. long, with a beam of 29ft. and a depth of 9.7ft. This picture, taken from the deck of a passing steamer, shows *Lady Moyra* carrying her full complement of passengers on a pleasant, calm day.

Right: The *PS Lady Margaret*, which was acquired by the FR in 1903 from P&A Campbell Ltd, to increase the frequency of services linking Barrow and Fleetwood. The steel-hulled vessel had been built in 1896 at Dumbarton for service in the Bristol Channel. With a length of 210ft., a beam of 25ft. a depth of 8.7ft. and a gross tonnage of 369, *Lady Margaret* was larger and faster than *Lady Evelyn*, but she was sold to the Admiralty in March 1908. The ship was built by A. McMillan & Son Ltd with engines by D. Rowan & Son.

Left: The *PS Philomel*, alternatively and affectionately known to local people as 'Full-o-Smell'; tied up at Barrow, awaiting her next sailing, while a group of men on the pier view my father with interest, as he took his photograph. This paddle steamer was acquired by the Furness Railway Company in April 1908, to replace the *PS Lady Margaret*, on the Fleetwood service. She was acquired from the General Steam Navigation Company and had been built in 1889 by J.Scott & Co., at Kirkcaldy. The vessel was 236ft. long, had a beam of 27.1ft. a depth of 9.5ft. and a gross tonnage of 564. *Philomel* was sold in 1913, after a period spent laid up.

Right: It would never be allowed today! On September 6 1913, the FR's overloaded paddle tug *Walney* wallows across Morecambe Bay, its paddle wheels completely awash, with a massive crowd aboard travelling from Barrow to Fleetwood to watch Barrow AFC play away to Fleetwood. Companion FR ships *Lady Moyra* and *Lady Evelyn* had both sailed with a full load apiece, leaving a large crowd still standing on the dock, hence this major overloading for *Walney*. *Lady Moyra* returned to Barrow for a second trip, this picture being taken as the larger paddle steamer passed the wallowing *Walney*, en route back to Fleetwood. Some passengers are standing on the wrong side of the rail, ahead of the paddle wheel, and quite how the skipper could see where he was going is a matter of conjecture. This was the second paddle tug to carry the name *Walney*: this vessel, as is clear from this picture, could carry passengers and was equipped with a forward saloon. The steel-hulled vessel had been built at South Shields in 1904 by J.P. Rennoldson & Sons and was fitted with simple steam engines. *Walney* was 120ft.long, with a beam of 21.1ft. and a depth of 10ft. Gross tonnage was 185. Around 1930 the tug was transferred by the LMS to Troon, where she took the place of a pair of Glasgow & South Western Railway tugs, and the vessel worked at Troon or Ayr as required. She was subsequently transferred to the Docks & Inland Waterways Executive and scrapped at Troon in 1952.

Right, below: The Morecambe Bay lightship, photographed from the open bridge of the *PS Lady Moyra*, on a calm day during a cross-Bay sailing prior to 1914.

THE ISLE OF MAN STEAM PACKET COMPANY

THE vessels of the Isle of Man Steam Packet Company are still a familiar sight in Morecambe Bay, as the Company's mainland operations today are based at Heysham. Formerly operating mainly between Douglas and Liverpool, the 'Steam Packet' shifted its English base in 1985 to Heysham, from where passengers and their vehicles are transported to the Isle of Man by modern 'roll-on roll-off' vessels.

The 'Steam Packet' has a long established practice of using traditional Manx names for its ships, and my father photographed ships in the Edwardian era which carried similar names to the modern vessels which maintain the Heysham-Douglas link in the 1980s.

In those days the IOMSP Company also sailed from Fleetwood — from whence sailings also operated to Northern Ireland — and many of his 'Steam Packet' pictures were taken from Fleetwood promenade. The late 19th century ships were coal-fired paddle steamers which frequently filled the air with rolling clouds of dense black smoke. This might not have been welcome to the Company's passengers, but it certainly made these beautiful ships even more impressive!

Above: The *PS Queen Victoria* churns to foam the waters of Morecambe Bay and demonstrates the prolific capacity for the production of thick smoke which it shared with identical sister ship *Prince of Wales*, shown below. Built by Fairfield, of Govan in 1887, *Queen Victoria's* statistics were similar to those of *Prince of Wales.*

Above: The furnaces are evidently well-stoked in this view of the *Prince of Wales*, which was built in 1887 by the Fairfield Shipbuilding & Engineering Company Ltd. The vessel was operated initially between Liverpool and Douglas by the Isle of Man, Liverpool & Manchester Steam Ship Company Ltd, which later sold *Prince of Wales* to the IOMSP Co. This handsome ship was driven by compound diagonal engines, each of two cylinders, and it is reported that *Prince of Wales* once covered the Liverpool Rock Light-Douglas Head sailing in 2hr 59 minutes — an average speed of 23¼ knots over 70 nautical miles. The Admiralty bought the ship in 1915 for net laying duties, and renamed it *Prince Edward.* The steel-hulled ship, (330.5ft. long x 39.1ft. beam x 15.2ft. depth) was eventually scrapped at Scheveningen, Holland.

Right: With the 'three legs of Man' carried proudly on her port paddlebox, the steel-hulled *PS Mona's Queen* steams out of Fleetwood with a full complement of passengers, bound for Douglas. The ship was launched at Barrow on April 18 1885 with a gross tonnage of 1,559. The hull was 328ft. long overall, with a beam of 38ft. 3in. and a depth of 14.5ft. Four double-ended boilers supplied steam to two sets of two-cylinder oscillating engines with a combined rating of 5,000 indicated horsepower. In 1888 *Mona's Queen* was fitted with new paddle wheels and equipment with superheating equipment by the Barrow Shipbuilding Company Ltd, which gave an increased IHP rating of 6239. During the First World War the vessel was use for troop transport and in 1917, en route from Southampton to Le Havre it rammed and sank a German U-Boat. On October 7 1929 the ship left Douglas bound for scrapping on the Clyde, the last 'paddler' in use by the 'Steam Packet.' This vessel had been acquired by the Steam Packet Company to replace an earlier vessel (a three-masted paddle steamer) of the same name, which had been built in 1852 and was withdrawn in 1880.

Right: The *PS Mona* gets under way from Fleetwood with a relatively sparse complement of passengers aboard, bound for the Isle of Man. This steel-hulled paddle steamer was launched on April 13 1889 by Fairfield, of Govan, for the London Chatham & Dover Railway Company, which named her *Calais-Douvres*. With a gross tonnage of 1,212, the ship had an overall length of 324ft., a beam of 35.9ft. and a depth of 13.5ft. In 1903 the vessel was bought by the IOMSP Co., which renamed it *Mona* — the third 'Steam Packet' ship to carry the name. It was the last paddle steamer to be acquired by the Company. *Mona* was broken up by T.W. Ward Ltd at Briton Ferry, South Wales, in 1909.

Above: The *Ramsey* under way in calm waters in the colours of the IOMSP Company, which acquired her from the Lancashire & Yorkshire and London & North Western Railway Companies, for whom she had been launched at Barrow as *The Duke of Lancaster*, on May 9 1895. This passenger steamer had a gross tonnage of 1,546 and was driven by steam engines of 5,340 IHP, its twin shafts giving the vessel a speed of 19 knots. *Ramsey* was 310ft. long, with a beam of 37 ft.

Right: The *TSS Viking* steams hard towards Douglas with a 'Steam Packet' sailing from Fleetwood, where the ship was a popular institution. A steel-hulled passenger steamer, *Viking* was launched on March 7 1905 by Armstrong Whitworth & Co.Ltd., of Newcastle; gross tonnage was 1,957 and the ship's overall length was 350.4ft., with a beam of 42ft. By 1905 the Parsons steam turbine had become firmly established as a reliable and powerful marine propulsion unit and *Viking* introduced this system to the 'Steam Packet' though the *Manxman*, owned by the Midland Railway, had been the first turbine steamer to visit the Isle of Man. The vessel's compound turbines were coupled directly to triple screws. *Viking* was also the only ship for the 'Steam Packet' to be built on the NE coast. It's top speed of 24 knots earned *Viking* an enviable reputation amongst the merchant steamers of the period — at the time only Cunard's mighty *Lusitania* and *Mauretania* liners were fast enough to outpace her! *Viking* had been built primarily for the Fleetwood service, because by this time the MR's Heysham service was well-established and the 'Steam Packet's' *Mona's Queen* was no match for the railway company's new speedy *Manxman*. *Viking* did however sail occasionally from Liverpool until the ship was purchased by the Admiralty for conversion as a seaplane carrier, in which role she served as *HMS Vindex* from 1915 to 1919 when the 'Steam Packet' re-acquired her and she returned to Fleetwood. *Viking* sailed from the Fylde Coast thereafter, the war years apart, until disposal, and the vessel was regarded as one of the most successful of the 'Steam Packet's' first class ships. In 1950–1, at the ripe old age of 46 years, *Viking* was overhauled and her turbines re-bladed, but she was sold four years later in October 1954 and after a distinguished and popular career the ship was scrapped at Barrow by T.W. Ward & Co.Ltd.

Left: The *TSS Snaefell*, which had been launched in 1904 as *Viper*, by Fairfield, for Messrs Burns, intended for their Ardrossan-Belfast service. The Irish 'troubles' prompted this company to dispose of *Viper*; the vessel was acquired by the 'Steam Packet' in March 1920 and renamed *Snaefell*. The vessel was 315ft. long with a beam of 39.6ft., a depth of 15.7ft., and a gross tonnage of 1,713. Triple steam turbines were directly coupled to the propellers. The vessel worked from both Heysham and Liverpool and it is reported that in the 1920s the *Snaefell's* skipper regularly took the vessel at full speed astern from the Liverpool Landing Stage to her moorings at the Sloyne! During World War 2 *Snaefell* shared the 'Steam Packet's' service (from Fleetwood only) with *Rushen Castle*. *Snaefell* was sold in 1945 for breaking up at Port Glasgow, but work did not start immediately. The ship's saloon staircase can now be seen in the *Wellington*, moored in the Thames, which is the headquarters of the Honourable Company of Master Mariners.

Above: The magnificent *Ben-My-Chree* of 1908,the longest, most powerful and fastest ship ever owned by the 'Steam Packet,' ordered by the Company in the wake of the *Viking*, in the aim of increasing the speed of service to Douglas. It was the third ship of the fleet to carry this name. Ordered in 1907 from Vickers and launched on March 23 1908, she was 389ft. long, powered by triple screw steam engines of 14,700 shaft horsepower and on trials achieved a maximum speed of 26.64 knots. This vessel's record passage from Liverpool Landing Stage to Douglas Head of 2hr. 58 min.still stands unchallenged. In 1915 *Ben-My-Chree* was one of six packet ships taken over by the Admiralty for conversion as seaplane carriers, modifications to *Ben-My-Chree* including alterations to the main deck and the construction of an aircraft hangar aft, being undertaken by Cammell Laird. High speed had been a prime consideration in the Admiralty's choice. Armed with six 12-pounder guns and carrying six seaplanes *Ben-My-Chree* went to war, firstly based at Harwich before being posted to the Dardanelles. On September 2 1915 *Ben-My-Chree* was in the news when she rescued 300 people from the torpedoed Red Star liner *Southland*, which she then towed into port. *Ben-My-Chree* also entered the war record as being the first ship to launch a successful air torpedo attack. On January 11 1917 she was shelled by a Turkish gun battery just off the island of Castellorizo, and sank after catching fire. The ship was successfully raised after the war, in 1919, but she was too extensively damaged to repair and she was sold for scrap at Piraeus, where she lay, in 1923. This picture shows *Ben-My-Chree* in original condition, demonstrating the high speed for which she was renowned.

Right: With her passenger decks deserted, the *TSS Snaefell*, the third vessel to carry this historic Manx name, steams slowly through the calm waters of Morecambe Bay on a murky day prior to 1914. Designed as a general purpose passenger and cargo steamer for the 'Steam Packet's' year-round Fleetwood Douglas service, *Snaefell* was launched by Cammell Laird, of Birkenhead, on February 2 1910, with an overall length of 269.8ft, a beam of 41.5ft, depth of 15.9ft. and a gross tonnage of 1,368. This was an extremely economical vessel, powered by two triple-expansion four cylinder engines, of 670 nominal horsepower. However *Snaefell* had a very short life and was torpedoed whilst on war service in the Mediterranean on June 5 1918.

Above: The *TSS Lady of Mann*, carrying the white livery applied to 'Steam Packet' ships in the 1930s is manoeuvred by tugs in Ramsden Dock, Barrow, following completion on June 12 1930. This ship was ordered on July 3 1929, laid down at Vickers on September 19 1929 and launched on March 4 1930 by the Duchess of Atholl. A handsome ship, the *Lady of Mann* (3,104 gross tonnage, 1,258 nett) was 372.3ft.long, with a beam of 50.2ft.and a depth of 17.4ft. Driven by four steam turbines and twin shafts of 12,500 shaft horsepower, *Lady of Mann* was capable of 22.5 knots. This ship was built as the centenary vessel of the 'Steam Packet' company and was remarkable for the short time of her construction — just less than nine months.

LYR/LNWR AND MR STEAMERS

In the early 1890s, railway shipping activity in Morecambe Bay was confined to Fleetwood and Barrow. The FR service between Barrow and Fleetwood has already been illustrated, but at Fleetwood were also based the ships of the Lancashire & Yorkshire Railway/London & North Western Railway joint concern. These steamers had black hulls, and black funnels with white bands, a livery dating back to the North Lancashire Steam Navigation Company of the middle 19th century. The LYR/LNWR flag was red, with a white superimposed St Georges Cross, on which was centred a three leaved shamrock. The lettering 'L&Y' and 'L&NWRy Coys' was carried in white at the corners of the flag. The MR started its shipping operations in Morecambe Bay with the opening of Heysham, in 1904 and its ships had black hulls, red 'boot toppings' (lower hull plating) and white superstructures, while the funnels had a black top, white mid-band and dark red lower sections.

Left: A brisk offshore breeze blows the thick smoke from the twin funnels of the *PS Duchess of Buccleuch* out across the Bay as she steams past in the early years of the century. Built as *Rouen* in 1888 by the Fairfield Shipbuilding & Engineering Co. at Govan, for the London, Brighton & South Coast Railway, this steel-hulled paddle steamer was acquired by the Barrow SN Co. (a joint company formed by the Furness and Midland railways and managed by Barrow shipping agents J. Little & Co.) in 1903 and renamed *Duchess of Buccleuch*. The ship was 250ft. long with a gross tonnage of 838, and was powered by two-cylinder compound steam engines. The vessel was disposed of in 1910.

Right: Built in 1893 by Laird Brothers of Birkenhead, for the Barrow Steam Navigation Company, *City of Belfast* (and later service companion *Duchess of Devonshire*) were the only screw steamers to be used regularly on passenger service between Belfast and Barrow. *City of Belfast* was introduced into service in 1893, with *Duchess of Devonshire* joining it four years later. Both ships were capable of 18 knots, driven by triple-expansion engines. Both ships became the property of the Midland Railway Company in 1907, after which they worked from Heysham. The LMS took over operation of the ships following the Grouping, in 1923, and in 1925 the ships were sold to Greek owners. *City of Belfast* was renamed *Nicolaos Togias*, later becoming *Kephallini*. *Duchess of Devonshire* was sold in July 1928,to M.H. Bland & Co, of Gibraltar, for £6,250, and renamed *Gibel Dersa*. She was eventually scrapped in 1949.

An impressive broadside view of *Duchess of Devonshire* (service companion to *City of Belfast*) which was launched at Barrow on January 21 1897 by the Duchess of Devonshire. The ship was built for the Barrow Steam Navigation Company as a dual-purpose vessel, designed to work the daylight Isle of Man service in the summer months and the Belfast-Barrow service in the winter. Temporary cabins were constructed in the saloons to provide the extra sleeping accommodation needed on the Barrow-Belfast duties. This ship was slightly larger than *City of Belfast*, and her triple-expansion engines of 4,922 indicated horsepower gave *Duchess of Devonshire* a speed of 18.37 knots.

Right: *TSS Duke of Connaught,* built in 1902 by John Brown & Co. Ltd, Clydebank, for the LYR/LNWR joint undertaking, makes slow headway into Fleetwood after a crossing from Belfast. This ship (gross tonnage 1,700) was the first steamer on the Fleetwood crossing to have a service speed of 20 knots. *Duke of Connaught's* maiden voyage took place in 1902 and the ship remained at Fleetwood from where she worked all three of her owners routes to Belfast, Londonderry and the Isle of Man. Railway steamers operated twice weekly to Londonderry, and were scheduled to sail from Londonderry and Fleetwood at 4pm and 8.45pm respectively, with the sea crossing generally taking 12 hours. This link was never particularly successful and the service was withdrawn in May 1912. In 1930 *Duke of Connaught* was transferred to Hull and worked for the next three years on the North Sea crossing to Zeebrugge, she was broken up in 1934.

Above: The Midland Railway's *TSS Antrim* built by John Brown & Co. Ltd, Clydebank, in 1904, passes through the bridge linking Barrow with Walney Island, probably after a visit to the Graving Dock, which could be drained to facilitate the cleaning of ships' hulls. The lifting bridge, completed in 1908, is apparently still under construction in this picture. *Antrim* was one of a fine trio of ships built to inaugurate the MR's new Heysham-Belfast service, started in 1904, and the 330ft long vessel had a gross tonnage of 2,000. Triple expansion four-cylinder engines drove twin screws and *Antrim* was capable of 20 knots. *Antrim,* and sister ships *Donegal* and *Londonderry,* were the first Irish traffic steamers to be equipped with wireless and they remained in service until displaced by the new 'Dukes' of 1928. All three vessels were very comfortable and after withdrawal by the LMS *Antrim* was required by the IOMSP Company which renamed her *Ramsey Town.* She was sold for scrap in 1935 and arrived at Preston for breaking on November 5 1936.

Above: Launched at Barrow on June 15 1904 for the Midland Railway, the 2,174-ton *TSS Manxman* was the best-known vessel of its time at Heysham and her 22.8 knot capability gave the MR ship a distinct edge over the 'Steam Packet's' *Mona's Queen.* The Manx Company answered by ordering the *Viking,* to match the MR's service. The 334ft long *Manxman* was fitted with triple screws, driven by three direct-coupled Parsons turbines, delivering 8,000 shaft horsepower. The first turbine steamer on the Manx service, *Manxman* was used for both daylight and night sailings from Heysham to Douglas. During World War I *Manxman* was taken over by the Admiralty and used from 1915 to 1918 as an auxiliary aircraft carrier; in 1920 the ship was purchased by the 'Steam Packet' and converted to burn oil fuel.

In 1939 *Manxman* was requisitioned as a troop transport ship, and served at Dunkirk: was later renamed *Caduceus* by the Admiralty and used as a radar training ship. For two years after World War II she carried repatriated PoWs from Harwich to the Hook of Holland, prior to arriving at Preston in September 1949, for scrapping.

Left: The LYR/LNWR *TSS Duke of Albany* (gross tonnage 2,259) built in 1907 by John Brown & Co. Ltd. Clydebank, was similar in appearance to the *Duke of Connaught,* built five years earlier for the same joint concern. Designed for the Fleetwood-Belfast service, *Duke of Albany* was driven by two sets of triple-expansion four-cylinder compound engines, fed with steam from five boilers fitted with forced-draught furnaces. The 330.5ft. long vessel was torpedoed in 1917.

TSS Duke of Argyll (and its sister ship *TSS Duke of Cumberland,* above, right) were the last passenger steamers built for the Belfast-Fleetwood crossing operated by the LYR/LNWR fleet. Built in 1909 by Denny & Brothers, Dumbarton, the *Duke of Argyll* had a working life of nearly two decades at Fleetwood. The ship had a gross tonnage of 2,100, was driven by turbines and was 330.9ft.long with a beam of 41ft and a depth of 17.1ft. In the late 1920s *Duke of Argyll* was transferred to Tilbury to work the newly-opened service to Dunkirk, operated by a French company in close association with the LMS, which took over the LYR/LNWR fleet with the railway Grouping. For this service the *Duke of Argyll* was renamed *Alsacien,* and was later transferred to work between Folkestone and Dunkirk until 1936, when the route was moved yet again to operate between Dover-Dunkirk. *Alsacien* then made a last sea crossing to a German shipbreakers.

Above: The *Duke of Cumberland,* sister ship to *Duke of Argyll,* approaches Fleetwood docks, flying on its aft mast the flag of the LYR/LNWR joint shipping concern — red background superimposed with a white St George's cross and a green shamrock. Also built by Denny's of Dumbarton in 1909, the ship was fitted with direct-drive steam turbines giving her a top speed of 21 knots. The turbines were laid out according to the practice of the day, with a high pressure turbine driving the centre propeller, and a pair of low pressure turbines driving wing propellers. The 'Dukes' were superb vessels, and when the LMS closed its Fleetwood service in favour of Heysham in 1928 *'Cumberland'* followed *'Argyll'* to Tilbury and Folkestone, where she was renamed *Picard* by her new operator, the Angleterre-Lorraine-Alsace Societe Anonyme de Navigation. Following the inauguration of the Dover-Dunkirk service in October 1936, *Picard* was sold to Greek owners and renamed *Heliopolis.* She was scrapped in 1936.

Left: At 3,600 gross tonnage, *TSS Duke of Argyll* was built for the LMS in 1928 to supersede the 'Dukes' of 1909, and at the time of their construction she and her sisters were the biggest vessels sailing on the Anglo-Irish service. Twin screws were driven by single reduction geared turbines using steam from coal-fired boilers. The vessel was built by Denny & Brothers, of Dumbarton, which also built sister ships *Duke of Lancaster* and *Duke of Rothesay*, and all three ships spent their peacetime careers on the Belfast-Heysham route, until they were replaced by three new 'Dukes' of the same names, in 1956. The 1928 'Dukes' were 349ft. long with a beam of 53ft. and a service speed of 21 knots.

Good passenger facilities were provided with berths for 400 saloon and 100 steerage passengers.

Sleeping cabins were on the promenade, bridge, main and lower decks. In World War II *Duke of Argyll* divided her time between trooping duties and normal working on the Anglo-Irish trade. *Duke of Argyll* was broken up at Troon in mid 1957.

Miscellaneous Steamers

Right: The small but attractive steam ship *Robina* on pleasure cruising duties in Morecambe Bay, with the uniformed master apparently sharing his completely open bridge with a handful of passengers. This steamer, built at Ardrossan in 1914 for the Morecambe Central Pier Company, with a gross tonnage of 306, was used for cruising between Blackpool and Morecambe during the summer season. *Robina* was 159ft. long, with a beam of 26.1ft and a depth of 8.8ft. She was used for a single season, circa 1920, in an attempt to revive the Barrow-Fleetwood service, but this was not successful. *Robina* was broken up in 1953.

Right, above: Carrying a substantial complement of passengers, the *PS Lune* enters Fleetwood, overlooked by the impressive 'North Euston Hotel' on the promenade. *Lune* was a small vessel added to the LYR/LNWR fleet in 1892 for service between Morecambe, Blackpool and Fleetwood. The steel-hulled ship (253 gross tonnage) was sold to Cosens & Co. Ltd, in June 1913, after which it was renamed *Melcombe Regis. Lune* was built in 1892 by T.B. Seath & Co. of Rutherglen, with compound diagonal steam engines by Rankin & Blackmore. The vessel was 129ft. long with a beam 24.1ft. and a depth of 9.1ft.

Right below: Built in 1892 as the *PS Belle of Llandudno* for the Llandudno & Caernarvon Steam Boat Company, this ship was transferred to the Lancashire coast in 1895, after which it was known simply as *Belle,* and was based at Blackpool. The vessel was built at Plymouth by Willoughby Brothers and was 143.7ft long, with a beam of 19.2ft. and a depth of 8ft. The gross tonnage was 147 and *Belle* was driven by four-cylinder compound engines. Seen here passing the Wyre Light and photographed from a passing ship, *Belle* was broken up in 1921.

Left: The Knott End steam ferry *Wyresdale* makes way with one of its short but important passages to Fleetwood — this little boat eliminated the need for a very lengthy road journey from Fleetwood to Knott End. *Wyresdale,* built in 1925 by James Robertson & Sons Ltd, carried out this unspectacular work for many years until her career was ended by a boiler explosion in 1957, after which she was withdrawn.

Above: Any study of Fleetwood would be incomplete without at least a glance at its once-busy trawler fleet. The departure of the fishing fleet at high tide was always an impressive sight. This picture shows FD 397 *Harry Melling,* a classic Fleetwood trawler, on its way out to sea, with clouds of black smoke indicating that the furnace is stoked to capacity! This vessel was a standard trawler of the 'Castle' class, built in 1919 by C. Rennoldson & Co. of South Shields, 125.3ft. long, with a 23.4ft. beam and a draught of 12.6ft. Gross tonnage was 275. Originally to have been named *John Lewis* the ship was renamed *John Evans* by the Admiralty before being sold out of Naval use to the Ministry of Agriculture & Fisheries. The trawler was registered in 1921 to Melling Trawlers Ltd, of Fleetwood and renamed *Harry Melling.* Around four further changes of ownership occurred prior to scrapping in 1955. In 1932. this vessel was just one of 144 trawlers using Fleetwood as a base: by 1939 this total had fallen to 99.

Left: A general view of the Fleetwood fish docks showing a few of the many dozens of trawlers which once comprised the town's deep-sea fishing fleet.

WARSHIPS AT BARROW

IN THE years leading to World War I, the Vickers shipyard at Barrow was very busy indeed with a wide variety of warship construction, both for the Royal Navy and for a number of overseas countries, including Japan, Russia, Brazil and Argentina. My father, with his interest in ships and his developing business, continued to photograph the ever-changing scene around the docks. The Sankey Collection therefore grew and matured into a valuable record of shipping activity at Barrow in the Edwardian era, and this first look at Barrow in its own right concentrates on the warships that were built on the Vickers slipways, and those which visited Barrow either for modification, repair, or breaking. At this time Britain's Naval power was immense, and Vickers at Barrow played a large part in the development of the fighting ship. In some instances, new innovations at Vickers showed the Royal Navy the way ahead — a proud tradition indeed.

Above: In addition to shipbuilding and repair, Barrow docks also hosted shipbreaking activities in the disposal of out-dated and life-expired vessels. *HMS Dreadnought* is seen here awaiting breaking by T.W. Ward & Co.'s yard, following sale for scrap by the Royal Navy, for £23,000, in 1908. Laid down at Pembroke Dockyard under the 1870 Naval Estimates, *HMS Dreadnought* was conceived as an enlarged version of *HMS Devastation,* but with more powerful machinery and a 'ram bow'. *HMS Dreadnought* was the last British battleship to have overall armour as a true 'Ironclad', and it carried the thickest complete armour belt of any British battleship. The hull armour was 14 inches thick at its thickest part. The ship was laid down in 1872, launched on March 8 1875 and completed on February 15 1879 at an overall cost of £619,739. *HMS Dreadnought* had a displacement of 10,886 tons, of which the hull and armour accounted for 7,286 tons and its other equipment 3,600 tons. The armour alone weighed 3,690 tons (nearly 34 per cent of the total tonnage) whilst the weight of guns and ammunition accounted for 400 tons. The ship had a crew complement of 369 and a total bunkerage for 1,800 tons of coal gave *HMS Dreadnought* a radius of 5,700 nautical miles at 10 knots speed. The total weight of her engines and machinery was 1,430 tons. *HMS Dreadnought* was regarded as a successful and popular battleship, which performed well with minimal 'roll' when under way. She was equipped with a twin-shaft two cylinder Humphreys & Tennant vertical compound engine and 12 cylindrical boilers which produced an output of 8,206 indicated horsepower and a top speed of 14.52 knots. *HMS Dreadnought's* armaments included: four 12.5in. guns,together with six 6pdr. and 12 3pdr. types. In 1884 ten machine guns were added, being replaced in 1894 by six 6pdr. and ten 3pdr. weapons. The ship was reboilered and her funnels lengthened in 1898. *HMS Dreadnought* was in front line service until 1894, after which it served as a coastguard vessel before being reclassified as a second class battleship in 1900. The ship was reduced to harbour service in 1902, and transferred to reserve in 1905 prior to scrapping in 1908. In this view, the short 38-ton muzzle-loading 12.5in. gun barrels have been removed from the large front and rear turrets, visible on the deck at each end of the main superstructure.

Left: A visitor to Barrow in 1912 was *HMS Hermione*, which came to provide a naval support crew at the ill-fated launch of the Vickers-built Naval Airship No 1, an event fully photographed by my father. *HMS Hermione* was one of a class of eight 'Astraea' 2nd class cruisers launched in 1892/3 as an improvement of the earlier 'Apollo' class ships. Displacement was increased by 1,000 tons to provide a hull of improved seaworthiness, fitted with heavier and better-placed armaments. Laid down in 1891 at Devonport Dockyard and launched on November 7 1893, *HMS Hermione* was completed on January 14 1896. The 339ft. 6in. long ship had a displacement of 4,360 tons (fully loaded) and was driven by twin-shaft three-cylinder engines, supplied with steam by eight cylindrical boilers, giving a speed on trials of 20.5 knots. The deck was protected by 2in.-thick armour and coal capacity was 1,000 tons. Guns fitted were: two 6in., eight 4.7in., ten 6pdr. and one 3pdr. weapon, together with four 18in. diameter torpedo tubes. *HMS Hermione* was sold in 1922 and renamed *Warspite* for use as a training ship. It was sold for scrap to T.W.Ward & Co. Ltd in September 1940.

Facing page, lower: *HMS Repulse* under tow during a visit to Barrow. Built in 1892 at Pembroke Dockyard, *HMS Repulse* was a 'Royal Sovereign' class battle ship of the type now known as 'Pre-Dreadnoughts'. The 380ft. long ship, (displacement of 14,150 tons), cost £915,302 and was powered by two sets of three-cylinder triple-expansion engines of 9,000 horsepower. Steam was supplied by eight cylindrical single-ended boilers working at 155 psi, giving a speed of 15.5 knots. *HMS Repulse* was the first British battleship to have steel armour and the first to exceed 12,000 tons displacement. The ship carried a maximum coal supply of 1,100 tons and a crew of 712 men. In addition to her main 13.5in. gun battery, *Repulse* was fitted with two submerged torpedo tubes in the bow, four further tubes above water abeam and one torpedo tube above the waterline astern. The ship was sold for scrap on July 11 1911 for £33,550.

Above: *HMS Powerful*, launched on July 24 1895 by the Duchess of Devonshire. At the time of completion, *Powerful* and its sister *HMS Terrible* were the largest warships in the world. Displacing 14,200 tons and 538ft. long, *HMS Powerful* had a beam of 71.5ft. and a maximum draught of 31ft. Two sets of triple-expansion four-cylinder engines drove twin shafts, using steam from 48 Belleville boilers, giving a speed of 21.8 knots. Bunker coal was normally 1,500 tons, with maximum capacity if required of 3,000 tons. Armaments included two 9.2in., 16 6in., and 16 3in. guns together with 12 3pdrs, two machine guns and four 18in. diameter torpedo tubes. The ship cost £850,000 to build, became the training ship *HMS Impregnable II* in 1919 and was scrapped in 1929. Although she was impressive on paper, *HMS Powerful* was something of a white elephant: she was expensive and fulfilled no true requirement of the Royal Navy.

HMS Vulcan was built in 1889 to carry six small, fast torpedo boats, used to launch attacks against enemy ships in the pre-submarine eras. Although *HMS Vulcan* might have experienced difficulty in re-loading its small craft in the aftermath of an attack and under fire, it was a promising ship, although it was regarded by parts of the military hierarchy as 'ungentlemanly' and 'unsporting'. She was a 'one-off', pictured here at Barrow, as converted to submarine depot ship, in 1915. Equipped with its own gun battery and torpedoes, *HMS Vulcan* was protected by 5in. deck armour. Capable of 20 knots, the 6,629-ton ship later became a hulk was scrapped in the mid 1950s.

Right below: The development of the fast torpedo boat was also pursued by potential enemies and the RN developed its own antidote to this threat in the shape of the torpedo boat destroyer. These vessels were like small, elegant cruisers, with a low profile and a high speed capability, for their role as guardians of the fleet. *HMS Cynthia* was a 'D' class TB destroyer built by Thornycroft in 1898, and is pictured here steaming down the Walney Channel after a visit to Barrow. Triple-expansion compound steam engines gave the 400-ton vessel a speed of 30 knots and it was armed with a single 12pdr and five 6pdr guns and two 18in. diameter torpedo tubes.

Left:Laid down in 1899 and launched on November 8 1900, the battleship *Mikasa* was built by Vickers for the Japanese Imperial Navy and completed in 1902. The 400ft.long vessel displaced 15,150 tons with a maximum draught of 27.2ft. and was powered by two sets of triple-expansion three-cylinder engines of 16,431 indicated horsepower. Twin shafts were fitted and *Mikasa* was capable of 18.5 knots and at full speed consumed 12 tons of coal per hour. A maximum of 1,690 tons of coal could be stowed aboard (700 tons normally) to fire 25 Belleville boilers. Guns fitted were: four 12in., 14 6in., 20 12 pdr., eight 3pdr. and four 2.5pdr. weapons together with four submerged torpedo tubes. During World War II *Mikasa* was blown up by Allied 'frogmen' but she was salvaged yet again and is now preserved in her original condition as a national monument in Japan.

Under tow in Buccleuch Dock is the battleship *HMS Triumph*, which had been laid down on March 13 1902 and launched in January 1903 as the *Libertad*, for Chile. The ship was purchased during fitting-out, on December 3 1903, by the Royal Navy for £937,500, and renamed *HMS Triumph*. The ship was completed in June 1904 with a displacement of 11,985 tons and an overall length of 470ft., a beam of 71ft. and a draught of 24.7ft. Steam from 12 Yarrow large tube boilers drove two sets of triple-expansion twin-shaft engines (rated at 14,093 indicated horsepower) giving a speed of 20.17 knots. Normal coal bunkerage was 800 tons, with maximum storage for 2,000 tons. *Triumph* had a crew of 700 and her guns included four 10in., 14 7.5in., 14 14pdr, two 12pdr and four pdr weapons, four machine guns, and a pair of 18in. diameter torpedo tubes. She was sunk on May 25 1915 by a torpedo fired by U21 off Gaba Tepe, in the Dardanelles.

Right: *HMS Dominion*, a 'King Edward VII' class battleship built at Barrow and completed in July 1905. The 16,350-ton displacement ship was laid down on May 23 1902 and launched on August 25 1903. Four-cylinder twin-shaft compound steam engines gave the 453.8ft. long ship a speed of 19.5 knots. Babcock boilers were fitted and the ship could bunker up to 2,150 tons of coal, though in normal circumstances 950 tons was carried. The ship cost about £1 million and was crewed by 776 men. Guns fitted were: four 12in., four 9.2in., 10 6in., 12 12pdr., and 14 3pdr. types, and two machine guns. Five 18in. diameter torpedo tubes were also provided. *HMS Dominion* served in the 3rd Battle Squadron in 1914, becoming a depot ship in 1917. On May 9 1921 she was sold to T.W. Ward for scrap and arrived at Preston for breaking on October 28 1924.

Left above: The Russian armoured cruiser *Rurik*, a ship which conveyed an impression of great power, launched at Barrow on November 17 1906 and completed in September 1908. The ship was built for the Imperial Russian Navy and she took the name of an earlier ship, launched in 1893, which displaced 10,923 tons and was capable of 18.5 knots. Speculation and alarm at the earlier ship's specification prompted the British Admiralty to build *HMS Powerful* and *HMS Terrible* to counter the supposed threat.

Left below: 'Warrior' class cruiser *HMS Natal* laid down on January 6 1904 at Barrow, launched on September 30 1905 by the Duchess of Devonshire and completed in 1907. The ship cost £1,162,366 to build and her sister ships were *HMS Achilles, HMS Cochrane* and *HMS Warrior.* With an overall length of 505.5ft. beam of 73.5ft. and a maximum draught of 27.5ft. *HMS Natal*'s actual displacement was 12,660 tons against a design figure of 13,550 tons. She attained 23.24 knots during trials, and *HMS Natal*'s machinery included 19 Yarrow and six cylindrical boilers, supplying steam to two sets of triple-expansion four-cylinder engines, driving twin shafts. The bunkers normally carried 1,000 tons of coal (total stowage for 2,050 tons) and 400 tons of oil. Guns fitted were: six 9.2in., four 7.5in., two 12pdr. field guns, and 25 3pdr. weapons, together with two machine guns, eight 'pom-poms', and three submerged 18in. diameter torpedo tubes. Crew complement was 704. *HMS Natal* was destroyed by an internal explosion at Cromarty Firth on December 30 1915. This picture shows the ship in original condition, in which the short funnels 'smoked out' the bridge: these were subsequently extended. At full speed the vessel burned 23.5 tons of coal per hour, or 15 tons at 21 knots.

Right: A very interesting view of Devonshire Dock, Barrow, viewed from the Michaelson Road bridge, with warships and merchant vessels — side by side. The picture was probably taken during 1907, as the two warships on the fitting-out berths are (left) *Rurik* (completed 1908) and *HMS Natal*, which was handed over to the Royal Navy in 1907. This stern-end view of the two warships emphasises the immensely powerful appearance of the Russian vessel, which had a beam of 75ft. and a displacement of 15,170 tons, compared with *HMS Natal*, which was only slightly narrower at 73.5ft.beam, but with a displacement of 12,660 tons. She was 490ft.long with a draught of 26 ft, driven by two sets of quadruple - expansion four-cylinder twin-shaft engines of more than 20,000 horsepower, which gave the *Rurik* a speed of 21.43 knots on trials, though considerable trouble was reported at this stage. Belleville boilers were fitted and normal coal stowage was 1,200 tons, with maximum bunkerage for 2,000 tons, if needed. Four 10in. guns were fitted together with eight 8in., 20 4.7in. and 14 smaller weapons, in addition to two 18in. diameter torpedo tubes. With a crew of 800 men, the vessel was renamed *Profintern* between 1921 and 1926, and it was scrapped circa 1930.

Above: The *General Guerrero*, built at Barrow for the Mexican government, steams slowly through Ramsden Dock, ready for delivery to the owner. Launched on January 23 1908 as a general purpose cruiser/transport ship, it was fitted with 1,200 horsepower steam engines giving a top speed of 14 knots. Six 4in.and 2 3pdr. guns were fitted to the ship, which was renamed *Vicente Guerrero* circa 1918.

Right: Although apparently complete, *HMS Vanguard* is not flying the White Ensign and is probably pictured during sea trials of October 1909, prior to delivery to the Royal Navy on March 1 1910. The ship had been laid down on April 2 1908 and launched on February 22 1909. Originally laid down as *HMS Rodney, Vanguard* was one of three 'St Vincent' class 'Dreadnoughts', the sister ships being *HMS St. Vincent* and *HMS Collingwood.* She cost £1,607,780 (including guns) and was completed in less than two years as the cheapest battleship of her period. *HMS Vanguard* served at the World War I Battle of Jutland in the 4th Battle Squadron and survived, only to be destroyed by an internal explosion at Scapa Flow on July 9 1917. This explosion, thought to be the result of faulty ammunition, resulted in the death of 804 of her crew: there were only two survivors in the fearsome blast.

Left: In the early years of the 20th century the Vickers yard was busy with warships for overseas customers, as well as the Royal Navy, including the battleship *Sao Paulo*, for Brazil. This ship is seen here on April 20 1909, under tow immediately after launch into the Walney Channel, on its short trip, via Ramsden Dock, to the fitting-out berths in Buccleuch Dock. The ship was laid down in June 1907 and completed in July 1910. *Sao Paulo* was a mighty ship indeed, similar in many ways to the Royal Navy's *HMS Dreadnought*, completed at Portsmouth in 1906 with Barrow-built engines. *HMS Dreadnought's* fearsome all big-gun battery of 10 12in. weapons rendered all previous battleships obsolete — and *Sao Paulo* was armed with 12 12in. guns, 22 4.7in. guns, eight 3 pdrs. and four torpedo tubes. The ship was ordered by Brazil to meet the threat posed by the new ships ordered by Chile, *Libertad* and *Constitucion* which actually became the Royal Navy's *HMS Triumph* and *HMS Swiftsure. Sao Paulo* illustrated Vickers' forward-thinking approach and showed the Admiralty the way ahead in many respects. The Furness Railway paddle tug *Lismore*, on the left of this picture, was a 181-ton (gross) vessel launched at Barrow on September 2 1874.

Sao Paulo's impressive 'Dreadnought' likeness is apparent in this view of the completed vessel, being manoeuvred in Buccleuch Dock ready to leave Barrow, following completion in July 1910. This view emphasises the ship's 12in. gun battery, which was mounted on superimposed twin turrets fore and aft, with two similar 'wing' turrets amidships, either side of the central superstructure. This layout enabled *Sao Paulo's* Captain to fire eight of the 12in. guns broadly ahead or astern, or to unleash a ten-gun broadside. With a length of 530ft, a displacement of 19,281 tons and a maximum draught of 28ft, *Sao Paulo* was driven by two sets of triple-expansion three-cylinder engines of 28,645 horsepower, giving a trials speed of 21.6 knots. Babcock boilers (18) and twin shafts were fitted and the vessel normally carried 800 tons of coal, with maximum bunkerage for 2,350 tons, plus additional fuel oil. At 10 knots, she had a steaming radius of 10,000 miles. A crew of 900 was needed and *Sao Paulo* cost the Brazilian Government £1,821,400. In 1917–1919 the ship was fully refitted at the New York Navy Yard, in readiness for a proposed detachment to the British Grand Fleet, but this never happened. *Sao Paulo* was decommissioned in 1946 and she deteriorated badly in subsequent years: no buyer was found and the ship was sold to British breakers in 1951. On September 20 1951 *Sao Paulo* left Rio de Janeiro under tow by tugs *Bustler* and *Dexterous*, on her last voyage to a British scrapyard, but on November 4 1951 she broke the towline 150 nautical miles north of the Azores. A search was continued until November 19, but *Sao Paulo* was never seen again.

Right: 'Bristol' class cruiser *HMS Liverpool* leaves Barrow, her crew lining the rail, following delivery to the Royal Navy on September 8 1910. The vessel had been laid down on February 17 1909, launched on October 30 1909 and underwent sea trials in June 1910, just 16 months after the keel plates were laid. The ship displaced 4,800 tons and was 453ft. long, with an average draught of 15.25ft. Driven by four shafts and Parsons turbines, *HMS Liverpool* recorded 26.09 knots on trials. Twelve Yarrow small-tube boilers were fitted and coal bunkerage was normally 600 tons, with total stowage for 750 tons. The ship cost £344,871 to build and needed a crew of 376. She was armed with two 6in., and ten 4in. guns, together with a single 3in. anti-aircraft gun and a pair of 18in. torpedo tubes. She served in the Grand Fleet at Heligoland Bight in 1914 and in the Mediterranean in 1915, ending the war at Constantinople in 1918. *HMS Liverpool* went to the breakers in Germany in 1921.

Right above: 'Weymouth' class cruiser *HMS Dartmouth* is manoeuvred by tugs in the docks at Barrow during fitting-out: the ship was launched on February 14 1911 by the Countess of Dartmouth and completed on October 16 1911, following sea trials held in the previous July. Originally conceived as Second Class Cruisers, the 'Bristol', 'Weymouth', 'Chatham' and 'Birmingham' class cruisers were general duty vessels intended to counter the ever-increasing classes of German light cruisers. *Dartmouth*, like all the 'Town' cruisers, had four funnels, of which the fore and aft were much slimmer than the centre pair. The majority of the 'Towns' saw service in World War I, *HMS Dartmouth* serving during 1914 in the Indian Ocean and the South Atlantic, moving in 1915 (via the Dardenelles in 1915) to counter the Austrian fleet in the Adriatic. On May 15 1917 she was torpedoed, but reached port safely and survived until withdrawal and scrapping in 1930. *HMS Dartmouth* was armed with eight 6in. guns, together with four machine guns, one 3in. anti-aircraft gun and a pair of submerged 21in. broadside torpedo tubes. A crew of 376 was needed and the ship cost £334,847, the cheapest of her class at just £63.7 per ton. Her trials speed was 25.9 knots.

Right, below: The traditional bottle of champagne has been smashed across the bow and 'Lion' class battle-cruiser *HMS Princess Royal* takes to the water in the Walney Channel for the first time on April 29 1911. Built for the Admiralty at a cost of £2,089,178, *HMS Princess Royal* was the largest and fastest capital ship laid down at this time. The 'Lion' class (sister ships *HMS Queen Mary* and *HMS Lion* were the first RN ships to cost more than £2 million each, and their construction entailed the biggest rise in displacement then recorded, to 29,680 tons.

Left: The 680ft. long hull of *HMS Princess Royal* has entered the water at Barrow on April 29 1911, where Furness Railway tugs *Furness, Cartmel* and *Walney* are waiting to tow the battle cruiser to its fitting-out berth as soon as the drag chains have been disconnected. *HMS Princess Royal* had a beam of 88.3ft., a maximum draught of 30ft. and was driven by Parsons turbines and four propeller shafts. Steam came from 42 Yarrow boilers and the vessel's 78,645 shaft horsepower resulted in a trials speed of 28.54 knots. Press reports gave an exaggerated average speed of 33.5 knots, with a maximum of 34.7 knots. However, as this would have required the engines to develop over 200,000 horsepower, the impossibility of the claim is clear, but it gave the public an inflated view of the abilities of the 'Lion' class.

Above: *HMS Princess Royal*, in complete condition and with her deck crowded, is towed stern-first down Buccleuch Dock, during trials prior to completion in November 1912. The gun turret aft carried two of the ship's eight 13.5in. guns, a second turret being sited in the gap between the funnels and two more turrets forward of the bridge. Other armaments included 16 4in., and four 3pdrs., together with five machine guns and three 21in. diameter torpedo tubes. Crew complement was 980. In 1914 *HMS Princess Royal* served with the 1st Battle Squadron at Heligoland Bight, and in 1915 at Dogger Bank. She was the Flagship of the Squadron at Jutland in 1916, recording nine hits. She was withdrawn under the terms of the Washington Treaty, and was sold for scrap on December 19 1922, arriving at Rosyth on August 13 1923. The breakers started work in 1926.

Right, above: The cruiser *Ying Swei* slips her towline in the Walney Channel, having being towed out of Ramsden Dock, and makes ready for sea. Built as a training vessel for the Chinese Navy, *Ying Swei* was launched on July 14 1911 and completed in 1912. She was 300ft. long, displaced 2,750 tons and was capable of 21 knots, driven by four shafts and Parsons steam turbines. Guns fitted were: two 6in., four 4in., two 14pdr. and six 3pdr. types, plus two 18in. diameter torpedo tubes. She was reported sunk by the Japanese at Canton on September 14 1937.

Left: A huge cloud of confetti showers over the watching crowds from the balloon suspended from the bow of the battle cruiser *Kongo*, during its launch on May 18 1912. At this time Japan was inexperienced in the techniques of large warship building, and needed a vessel built abroad to act as a prototype, from which to build its own ships. *Kongo*, built by Vickers at the same time as the Admiralty 'Lion' class battle cruisers (see *HMS Princess Royal*, page 24-5), was the result, designed by British Naval Architect Sir George Thurston. The 'Lion' class was the Admiralty's own design, but *Kongo* was the product of in independent, free-thinking and innovative shipyard: the end result was a ship which outclassed *HMS Lion* and her sisters. Consequently, the planned fourth ship of the 'Lion' class, *HMS Tiger*, was modelled on the *Kongo* and appeared as the first British warship with an engine output in excess of 100,000hp and the last capital ship with coal-fired boilers. Such was the influence of the *Kongo*.

Kongo is clearly approaching completion in this view of the ship, tied up at the fitting-out berth in Buccleuch Dock. The fires are lit, the guns fitted and the ship is apparently being painted, ready for completion in August 1913. Laid down in 1911, *Kongo's* initial loaded displacement was 27,900 tons, though subsequent rebuilding by the Japanese increased this to 32,156 tons. The ship was 704ft.long, with a beam of 91.9ft and 29.5ft maximum draught. Built for a crew of 1,100 this was later increased to 1,437, and the *Kongo* cost £2,500,00 — a sum which in the 1980s would buy perhaps a couple of miles of Motorway! On the dockside a train of materials is in the charge of Manning Wardle 0–6–0ST *Cyclops*, one of a fleet of steam locomotives privately owned by Vickers for internal duties.

Kongo at sea, probably during trials. Comparison with *HMS Princess Royal* shows how the third turret has been moved aft of the third funnel, giving the 14in. guns a clearer line of fire aft. Steam from 36 Yarrow boilers powered Parsons turbines, built by Vickers, driving four shafts and developing 78,275 shaft horsepower, giving a speed on trials of 27.53 knots. Normal coal bunkerage was 1,000 tons, with total stowage if required for 4,000 tons. At the time of her construction *Kongo* was undoubtedly the best battle cruiser afloat. Rebuilding in the late 1930s increased her speed to 30.5 knots, and increased her range (at 18 knots) to 9,800 nautical miles. *Kongo* was torpedoed and sunk on November 21 1944, by an American submarine off North-West Formosa.

Above: With the furnaces being stoked ready for the battle cruiser to make way under her own power, *Kongo* is towed through Ramsden Dock, during sea trials. Although *Kongo* suffered, like many other British-built ships of the period, from inadequate armour protection, she was a formidable vessel and during 1916/17 the Admiralty attempted to borrow or buy *Kongo* and her three Japanese-built sisters (*Hiei, Haruna* and *Kirishima*) to serve in both the Mediterranean and the North Seas, but the Japanese refused to agree.

Left: The lifting railway bridge at the west end of Buccleuch Dock stands in salute as *Kongo* is towed slowly through on its way to sea, though the piles of clutter on deck and the men in civilian dress aboard indicate that this was during trials, and not for final delivery. The massive gun turret dominating the smaller calibre weapons carried 14in. guns (compared with the 13.5in. guns fitted to the 'Lion' class) fitted to keep pace with American developments. *Kongo's* original weaponry included: eight 14in., 16 6in., 16 14pdrs. five machine guns and eight submerged 21in. diameter torpedo tubes.

Above: Moored side-by-side in Devonshire Dock are the three 'River Monitor' flat-bottomed craft originally launched for the Brazilian Government as *Javary*, *Solimoes* and *Madeira*, in 1913, but which were bought by the Royal Navy when war broke out in 1914 and renamed *HMS Humber*, *HMS Severn* and *HMS Mersey* respectively. All three ships were launched in 1913 : *Javary* on June 17, *Solimoes* on August 19 and *Madeira* on September 30. These distinctive vessels had the rare distinction of being launched broadside into the Walney Channel. Although broadside launches were not uncommon at shipyards whose slipways adjoined narrow waters, Vickers normally favoured stern-first launches. One of the 'Monitors' can be seen (right, above) under construction on its multiple slipway, and (right, below) as it takes to the water for the first time, a paddle tug standing by to take her in tow for the short journey through Ramsden Dock to the fitting-out berths in Devonshire Dock. The 'Monitors' displaced 1,260 tons and were 266.8ft. long with a beam of 49ft. and an average draught of 5.7ft. Powered by triple-expansion steam engines of 1,450 indicated horsepower, they were designed for 12 knots and were designed for a crew of about 100 and a radius of action of 2,800 miles. Original armament was: two 6in. guns, two 4.72in. howitzers and a 4pdr. anti-aircraft gun. *HMS Humber* saw action in World War I off the Belgian coast and at the Dardanelles, being sold for scrap in 1920. On July 11 1915 *HMS Severn* and *HMS Mersey* engaged and sank the German cruiser *Königsberg* in the Rufiji River, East Africa, with gunfire being directed from the air for the first time. *HMS Severn* was sold for scrap together with *HMS Mersey* in 1921.

Above: The battleship on the right had three different names before she was completed, in August 1914, as Europe went to war. It had originally been laid down for Turkey as *Sultan Mehmet Rechad V* in December 1911, was launched on September 3 1913 as the *Reshadieh*, but was bought by the Admiralty on Churchill's orders prior to completion and renamed *HMS Erin*. The ship served with the 2nd Battle Squadron at Jutland in 1916, and was placed in reserve in 1919. *HMS Erin* was 560ft. long with a maximum draught of 28.5ft. and a displacement of 25,250 tons. Four shafts driven by Parsons turbines gave *Erin* a speed of 21.5 knots, and her bunkers could hold 900 tons normally (2,000 tons if needed) plus 710 tons of fuel oil. The ship was designed for a crew of 1,070 and her guns included ten 13.5in. and 16 6in., types, while four 3in. (anti-aircraft) guns were added later. She also had three 21in. diameter submerged torpedo tubes. After a relatively short life *HMS Erin* was on December 19 1922 sold to Cox & Danks for scrap at Queensborough. The ship was withdrawn under the terms of the Washington Treaty of 1921, which sought to limit naval fleets.

'Royal Sovereign' class battleship *HMS Revenge* cutting through the water at speed during trials. Originally laid down as *HMS Renown* on December 22 1913, the ship was launched on May 29 1915 and completed in March 1916. Displacement was 31,200 tons and steam turbines developing 40,000 shaft horsepower, and four shafts gave the ship a speed of 21.9 knots. Weaponry fitted included eight 15in., 14 6in., two 3in. (anti-aircraft) and four 3pdr. guns. Crew complement was 915. The original design provided for the burning of both oil and coal, but the vessel was actually completed as an oil burner only. At the time of construction *HMS Revenge* was the biggest warship built at Barrow (she displaced 6,000 tons more than *HMS Erin*) and she was the last battleship built at the yard.

Right: After being towed stern-first out of Ramsden Dock into the Walney Channel, a pair of tugs push against the bow of *HMS Medway*, to turn the ship so that she faces south, ready to steam away under her own power. A submarine depot ship, *HMS Medway* was launched on July 19 1928 and completed on July 6 1929. The ship was 580ft long and displaced 14,650 tons with an average draught of 19.9ft. A pair of Vickers-MAN eight-cylinder diesel engines of 8,000 brake horsepower and twin shafts gave the vessel a speed of 15 knots, and the engines were the first of their type to be built in Britain. *HMS Medway* carried 530 tons of fuel oil for her own engines, and a further 1,900 tons for refuelling submarines. A crew of 400 was needed and further accommodation was provided for 135 officers and 1500 men. Two 4in. and four 4in. (anti-aircraft) guns were fitted. In 1939 *HMS Medway* became the depot ship on the China station, moving to the Mediterranean in 1940. She was torpedoed and sunk off Alexandria on June 30 1942.

Above: 'C' class Destroyer *HMS Crescent* was being tested for manoeuvrability when this picture was taken during trials in Morecambe Bay. This ship was launched on September 29 1931 with a displacement of 1,375 tons and fitted with twin-shaft geared turbines of 36,000 shaft horsepower, giving a top speed of 35.5 knots. Armaments fitted: four 4.7in. and two 2pdr. anti-aircraft guns, together with eight 0.5in. machine guns and eight 21in. torpedo tubes. Crew complement was 145. *HMS Crescent* was one of a number of ships subsequently sold to the Royal Canadian Navy, for whom she served as *HMS Fraser* until she was sunk following a collision off Bordeaux on June 25 1940.

Right, above: With the White Ensign fluttering on the stern, 'B' class Destroyer Leader *HMS Keith* shows a brisk turn of speed during trials on a calm but misty day following completion on March 20 1931. Laid down in October 1929, the vessel was launched on July 10 1930 at 323ft. in length, with a beam of 32.2ft. and draught of 8.5ft.

Right, below: On April 8 1932, 'D' class Destroyer *HMS Diamond* floats for the first time in the Walney Channel, six months after being laid down on September 31 1931. Of 1,375 tons displacement, *HMS Diamond*'s 36,000 shaft horsepower steam turbines gave her a speed of 35.5 knots and she was armed with the same weaponry as *HMS Crescent*. This ship was bombed and sunk by aircraft during the evacuation of Greece on April 27 1941.

Above: the sleek profile of 'F' class Destroyer *HMS Fame*, undergoing trials in Morecambe Bay. Launched on June 28 1934 and completed on April 26 1935 *HMS Fame* had a fully loaded displacement of 2,060 tons, a length of 329ft.and an average draught of 8.5ft. The ship was capable of a maximum speed of 36 knots and was fitted with three Admiralty three-drum boilers feeding steam to Parsons geared turbines. At 15 knots *HMS Fame* had an operational radius of 6,000 miles and carried 480 tons of fuel oil. Four 4.7in. guns were fitted, together with eight 0.5in. machine guns and eight 21in. diameter torpedo tubes. In February 1949 the ship was sold to the Dominican Republic and renamed *Generalisimo*.

Above, left: The launch of a Royal Navy ship with a famous history. On March 1 1934 'Leander' class cruiser *HMS Ajax* glides into the water at Barrow, just over a year after the keel had been laid, on February 7 1933. The 6,985 ton displacement ship was completed on June 3 1935. *HMS Ajax* was 554.5ft. long and driven by Parsons geared turbines of 72,000 horsepower, the four shafts producing a top speed of 32.5 knots. Steam was supplied by four Admiralty three-drum boilers. Two aircraft, with catapult, were fitted and armaments included eight 6in., four 4in. (anti-aircraft), and four 3pdr. guns together with ten machine guns and eight 21in. diameter torpedo tubes. The crew of 550 became famous when *HMS Ajax* was involved in the destruction of the *Graf Spee*, vividly recorded in the film 'The Battle of the River Plate.' She was in the Mediterranean Fleet 1940–2 and was refitted in the USA in 1943 before spending a further two years in the Mediterranean, until 1945. She was scrapped at Newport by John Cashmore Ltd, with breaking starting in November 1949.

Above, right: Launches and other special occasions at Vickers often produced visits by senior Naval or Admiralty officers, or, as in this case, members of the Royal Family. Here we see the Duke and Duchess of York, aboard *HMS Ajax* on May 4 1935, the year before the abdication of his brother Edward VIII, which resulted in the Duke of York becoming King George VI. The Duchess of York of 1935 is better known in the 1990s as Queen Elizabeth the Queen Mother.

In the 1930s Vickers was still building warships for overseas customers and this was the *Buenos Aires*, a destroyer laid down in 1936 for the Argentine Navy. She was completed on April 4 1938 and is seen here being towed down Buccleuch Dock, probably during trials. *Buenos Aires* cost £400,000 to build and displaced 2,010 tons, fully loaded. Her top speed was 35 knots.

Above: An impressive sight, photographed from the lock gates at the entrance to Ramsden Dock, as a trio of destroyers (disp. 1,375 tons) built for Argentina are towed from the Walney Channel, immediately after launch, (September 21 1937) to the fitting-out berths in Buccleuch Dock. The destroyers have been admitted into the lock and are awaiting closure of the rear gates. The ships are (left to right) *Entre Rios*, *Buenos Aires* and *Corrientes*. All three vessels were laid down in 1936 and completed in mid-1938. The *Corrientes* was sunk on October 3 1941 following a collision during exercises with the heavy cruiser *Almirante Brown*.

Right: The drag chains pull tight, bringing aircraft carrier *HMS Illustrious* to rest in the Walney Channel, on launch day April 5 1939. *HMS Illustrious* could carry 36 aircraft and she was armed with 16 4.5in., 48 2pdr. (anti-aircraft) and eight 20mm (anti-aircraft) guns. The ship needed 1,392 crew and Vickers tender was for the hull to cost £1,690,000 with the machinery (also to be built at Barrow) adding a further £705,000. *Illustrious* left Barrow on April 20 1940, when she accidentally sank the tug *Poolgarth*. *Illustrious* was a very well-armoured ship and her aircraft hangar was a fortified box, completely enclosed within the hull. The flight deck was constructed of 3in. plate designed to withstand the impact of a 500lb. semi-armour piercing bomb dropped from below 7,500 ft. The hangar sides and ends were of 4in. armour capable of withstanding 6in. gunfire at ranges greater than 7,000 yards. The bridge was shielded with bullet-proof plating and the magazines and machinery were protected by 3in armour. *HMS Illustrious* needed a high speed (31 knots) in order to create the high airspeed over the flight deck needed by her aircraft, also the ability to turn quickly into the wind. Six three-drum boilers, in three groups of three in separate boiler rooms, provided steam for three sets of Parsons geared turbines, all built at Barrow. Sea trials revealed some vibration but this didn't become troublesome until the closing months of the war when the ship was beginning to show signs of hard usage and war damage. She served in the Mediterranean Fleet during 1940–41, launching a successful attack on Taranto on November 11/12 1940. She served with the Eastern Fleet 1942–43, with Force 'H' in 1943, the Eastern Fleet in 1944 and the Pacific Fleet in 1945. *HMS Illustrious* had a distinguished war record, her armoured deck affording considerable protection. She was scrapped at Faslane, where she arrived for breaking on November 3 1956. (See also page 5).

SUBMARINES

AS THIS BOOK went to press it was announced by the Ministry of Defence that *HMS Vanguard*, Britain's first nuclear-powered 'Trident' submarine is to be built at Barrow. Good business for the Vickers yard certainly, but it also maintains Vickers' role at the forefront of submarine design and construction, for the Navy's first submarines were built at Barrow at the turn of the century. When my father was busy with his camera the submarine service was in its infancy and the strange new craft must have appeared very odd indeed to the people of Barrow, who were at that time more accustomed to big-gun battleships and paddle-steamers.

The Royal Navy started negotiations in 1900 to acquire the 'Holland' design of submarine, which had been tested by the United States Navy, and two years later Vickers signed an exclusive contract with the Admiralty for the construction of submarines, which lasted until 1912. There was of course no 'track record' for this entirely new branch of naval activity; 'trial and error' was very much the order of the day, and there were inevitably mishaps and accidents along the way. Vickers has built many submarines over the years, not only for the Royal Navy but also for overseas customers, and in 1960 Barrow men scored another 'first' when, on October 21, *HMS Dreadnought*, Britain's first nuclear submarine, was launched into the Walney Channel. This section illustrates some of the pioneering vessels from the earliest days, a handful of the vessels launched in the closing months of World War I and several of the much larger submarines of the 1920s and 1930s — important milestones on the route to the 'Trident' order of 1986!

Left: Early officers of the submarine service take a turn around the docks on the deck of Holland No.2, launched at Barrow on January 21 1902. The 'Holland' vessels Nos. 1–5 were very similar to America's 'A' class and they were 63.3ft. long with a circular section of 11.8ft. These vessels displaced 104 tons on the surface and 120 tons submerged, and were driven by a single-shaft American-built petrol engine of four-cylinder vertical design. On the surface this produced 160 brake horsepower and a speed of 8 knots, with a single supplementary electric motor producing a submerged rating of 74bhp and a speed of 5 knots. Holland No.2 carried a crew of seven men and was fitted with a single 14in torpedo tube in the bow. The original design also specified an 8in. 'dynamite' gun on the bow, with an 11.25ft.long barrel, capable of firing a 22lb. projectile, but these were not actually fitted. Many lessons were learned from these early craft, which were difficult to control both under water and on the surface, and improvements carried out immediately to the basic design resulted in the following 'A' class. All five 'Holland' submarines had been disposed of by 1913, No. 2 being sold that year. This picture is evidently a posed event, with the crew turned out very smartly indeed.

The 'A' class was the first Admiralty-designed submarine and Nos. A1–A14 were all built at Barrow. In this view, submarine A3 is under way on trials in Morecambe Bay with six of its 11-man (sometimes 14-man) crew taking the air. No. A3 was launched on May 9 1903 and displaced 165 tons on the surface, 180 tons submerged. The craft was 100ft.long with a circular section of 11.5ft, powered by a single 16-cylinder Wolseley petrol engine (later modified to 12-cyl) and a single propeller shaft. On the surface A3 had a top speed of 11 knots whilst an electric motor made 7 knots possible whilst submerged. Two 18in. diameter torpedo tubes were fitted. The 'A' class was a great improvement on its 'Holland' predecessors, but a major problem was that the class was prone to dive without warning and No. A8's entire crew drowned in such an incident, although the vessel was subsequently raised. The use of petrol engines also resulted in several explosions, attributed to vapour build-up. A3 sank after a collision off Portsmouth with *HMS Hazard* on February 2 1912: the vessel was subsequently raised and used as a target, finally sinking in May 1912.

Right: HMS C10 is anchored to a buoy at Barrow, probably during trials. The submarine was launched at Barrow on April 15 1907 for the Royal Navy, and displaced 290 tons (surface) and 313 tons (submerged). It was 143ft.long, with a beam of 13.5ft.and a draught of 12ft, powered by a single 16-cylinder petrol engine driving one propeller shaft. Surface speed was 14 knots and underwater speed 10 knots. A crew of 16 was needed and the vessel had an operational radius of 1,500 miles, at 8.5 knots surface speed. A pair of 18in. torpedo tubes were fitted in the bow of C10, which was scrapped in 1921.

Left: HMS C31, launched at Barrow on September 2 1909, lies alongside *HMS Forward*, a light cruiser built in 1906 by Fairfield Govan. This vessel was of a type known as 'scouts' in this period, which acted as 'the eye of the Fleet' whilst at sea.

Right: A trio of 1918-built submarines, of class 'L', 'H' and 'R' are moored side-by-side in Devonshire Dock, providing an interesting comparison of designs. On the left is No. L12, launched at Barrow on March 16 1918 as a patrol submarine with a surface speed of 17 knots, and a submerged speed of 10.5 knots. Powered by a 12-cylinder four-stroke engine, this vessel could dive to a depth of 150ft.and was designed for a crew of 38. It carried 10 torpedoes, which could be fired from four 21in. tubes mounted in the bow, or two 18in. tubes fitted abeam. L12 was scrapped in 1932. The centre vessel is 'H' class No.H28, launched on March 12 1918, and scrapped at Troon in August 1944. It could dive to 150ft.and its underwater speed was 10 knots. Its range underwater was 70 miles at 3 knots, or nine miles at 8 knots. On the surface H28 could travel at 13 knots, at which speed it had a range of 1,100 miles. The vessel carried a crew of 22 and was armed with six torpedoes, which could be fired through four 21in. diameter tubes. On the right is 'R' class No. R7, launched on May 14 1918, as a 'first generation' hunter-killer submarine. Designed for a high underwater speed of 15 knots, the vessel had a crew of 22. Six 18in. diameter torpedo tubes were fitted and one 4in. deck gun. The class was not completed until late in the war and only one 'R' class submarine made an attack firing its full six torpedo salvo and missed its target. R7 was scrapped in 1923.

Left: 'O' class submarine *HMS Otus* in the Walney Channel immediately after launch, pictured from one of the dockside cranes, on August 31 1928. The submarine was 283ft. long with a displacement of 1,475 tons (surface) and 2,030 tons (submerged), and respective speeds of 17.5 knots/9 knots. *Otus* was armed with one 4in. gun, a pair of machine guns and eight 21in. diameter torpedo tubes. Crew complement was 53. *HMS Otus* served in the East Indies, moving in 1940 to the Mediterranean, Home Waters in 1942, and the South Atlantic (for training purposes) in 1943: the class suffered from leaks and was not successful. The vessel was scuttled off Durban in 1946.

Below: The tug *Cartmel* stands ready in the Channel as the Chilean Navy's submarine *Capitan O'Brien* is launched on October 2 1928, three of its six bow-mounted 21in. diameter torpedo tubes clearly visible. Two further tubes were mounted in the stern. This vessel, built to the 'O' class design, was the 150th submarine to be launched at Barrow and was completed on June 19 1929.

Above: 'P' class submarine *HMS Pandora* is launched on August 22 1929. Originally laid down as *HMS Python*, this vessel was completed on June 30 1930, with a displacement of 1,475 tons (surface) and 2,040 tons (submerged). Diesel-electric twin-shaft power units gave *Pandora* a surface speed of 17.5 knots and a submerged speed of 9 knots. The boat had a crew of 53 and weaponry included two machine guns, one 4in. gun and eight 21in. diameter torpedo tubes (Six in the bow, two in the stern). After serving in Chinese waters and going to the Mediterranean in 1940 *Pandora* was bombed and sunk in Malta on either March 31 or April 1 1942. The wreck was raised in 1943 and she was dismantled in 1957. The 'P' class submarines had a range of 8,500 nautical miles on the surface at 10 knots.

Right: 'Thames' class submarine *HMS Severn* awaits movement to its fitting-out berth after launch at Barrow on January 16 1934. It is said that these large boats were very comfortable for their 61-man crews. *HMS Severn* displaced 1,850 tons (surface) and 2,723 (submerged) with respective top speeds of 22.25 and 10 knots. The hull was 345ft. long, and was driven by twin-shaft diesel electric units giving 10,000 brake horsepower on the surface, and 2,500bhp whilst submerged. Armaments included one 4in. gun, two machine guns and eight 21in. torpedo tubes. The cost of this vessel was estimated at £500.000 and during the war it was based at Freetown until transfer to Home Waters in 1941, after which it served in the Mediterranean. In 1946 she was scrapped at Bombay.

BUILDING

THE LINERS

THE ORIENT STEAM NAVIGATION COMPANY

UNTIL the development of the jet aero engine made long-haul transportation by air possible, passengers and cargo destined for journeys across the world's oceans travelled on the beautiful and elegant 'liners,' many of which were built in Barrow. Cunard, the Orient Line and the P&O Steam Navigation Company all came to Vickers for some of their ships and I was fortunate to photograph these famous vessels in the inter-war years.

As with its warship construction, Vickers was in the forefront of the design and construction of civil and merchant ships and the vessels it turned out sailed the world's oceans for many years, with some vessels distinguishing themselves when requisitioned to serve their country during World War II.

Above: With the hull of the *Orama* towering above them, a small group of shipyard workers puts the finishing touches to the slipway prior to the launch of the vessel on May 20 1924. *Orama's* massive twin screws were turned by six Parsons steam turbines, generating 19,500 shaft horsepower, giving the 19,777 tons (gross) ship a speed of 19.75 knots. This was the second Orient Line steamer to carry the name *Orama*. She was urgently required by the company as World War I had left just four of its ships in service, and it marked the start of a working relationship with Vickers which stretched to the building of the *Oriana* in the late 1950s.

Left: Final preparations around the bow of the *Orama* for its launch included the construction of a special platform for the launch party, one of whom would send the ship down the slipway with the customary bottle of champagne, and a second platform from which press photographers such as myself could photograph the ceremony. The launch platform is visible on the right, with the press platform located alongside the workers access ramp.

Right: Launches were always spectacular, but *Orama*'s launch had special significance and was particularly important for Vickers and the people of Barrow, as it marked the end of a lengthy 'slump'. The ship had five decks and seven holds and was fitted with six double-ended and four single-ended boilers which were oil-fired and worked at 215psi.

Above: With the launch formalities over, *Orama* was towed through Ramsden Dock to a fitting–out berth in Buccleuch Dock, where her luxurious furnishings and fitments were added. This picture shows *Orama* nearing completion in Buccleuch Dock, the steam being vented from the rear of the second funnel indicating that the boilers are being tested. The ship was 632ft. long with a beam of 75ft. and a draught of 47ft, with accommodation for 592 first class, and 1,244 third class passengers: *Orama* was one of the few British mail steamers to be built without an interposed second class. Her accommodation was subsequently altered to suit changing circumstances and styles.

Left: With construction work and trials complete *Orama* is towed stern-first through the Ramsden Dock entrance lock, and out into the Walney Channel for delivery to her owner. A huge crowd of people were on the dockside on the left, to bid her farewell.

Orama steams away from Barrow, to start work for the Orient Line. A popular ship in service, *Orama* was requisitioned for war service in 1939 and converted for trooping duties. She was engaged on the evacuation of troops from Narvik, in Norway, when on June 8 1940 she was caught by the German battle cruiser *Admiral Hipper*, which opened fire and sank *Orama*, killing 20 of her crew. The *Hipper* picked up 240 survivors.

Above: A busy scene in Buccleuch Dock in late summer 1935, with the Orient Steam Navigation Company's *Orford* (launched on September 27 1927) being towed past the same company's *Orion* (launched on December 7 1934). The ship on the right is the P&O Steam Navigation Company's *Strathmore*, launched in April 1935 and seen here during fitting-out. *Orford* still carried the Orient Line's traditional black hull with white superstructure livery, whereas *Orion*, completed in July 1935, has her hull painted in the tan shade adopted by the company in the mid-30s. Driven by twin-shafts and with a speed of 19.75 knots, *Orford* was requisitioned for trooping in World War II and the ship was so seriously damaged by air attack at Marseilles on June 1 1940 that she was beached and allowed to burn out. She was a total loss. In this view, one of the Isle of Man Steam Packet Company's vessels is moored on the left, and the tugs are *Ramsden* (right) and *Devonshire*.

Above: The speeches and blessing have been said and the bottle of champagne is about to strike the bow of Orient Liner *Orcades* at her launch on December 7 1936, photographed from our specially-constructed press platform.

Right: *Orcades* at rest in the Walney Channel, shortly after launch. Note the securely mounted drag chains attached to the lower hull plating, designed to prevent the ship surging too far out into the narrow confines of the Channel. The last thing the Vickers management needed at such a prestigious occasion was the vessel 'beaching' on the other side of the Channel!

Left: In July 1937, ready for delivery to the Orient Line, *Orcades* is manoeuvered in the dock area by tugs en-route to the Walney Channel and the open sea. The 664.5ft. long ship was driven by six steam turbines (of 24,000 shaft horsepower) to give a top speed of 20.5 knots. *Orcades* carried 550 first class and 700 tourist class passengers, and in the war was used for trooping in the Middle East, also rescuing civilians from the Dutch East Indies in February 1942. En route for Britain in October 1942, and 217 miles out of Capetown, she was hit by a total of six torpedoes fired by the German submarine U 172, which dived mid-attack to reload, actually firing its torpedoes in three groups of two, one and three. *Orcades* sank with the loss of 48 people, though the Polish ship *Narwik* picked up 950 survivors on October 10.

The Orient SN Company's *Orion* has been turned through 90 degrees in the Ramsden Dock basin by the two tugs on the left, and the tug just visible on the right is taking the strain to tow the 23,371 gross tons ship out through the entrance lock and into Walney Channel, following completion in July 1935. The launch of *Orion* on December 7 1934 had been a technological milestone as the launch speech by HRH the Duke of Gloucester was beamed by radio from Brisbane, Australia, after which he pressed a button which, from the other side of the world, simultaneously tripped the champagne bottle release and the launch triggers, sending the ship down the slipway. Trans-global communications are now taken for granted but in 1934 it seemed like a miracle. She was capable of 20.5 knots and during the war served as a troopship, returning to passenger service in 1947, having taken part in the North African landings of 1942. She was sold by the Orient Line in 1963 for use as a floating hotel in Hamburg, but was scrapped later the same year.

Top: Launched on October 14 1947 and completed in November 1948, this new *Orcades* was built by the Orient SN Company to replace the vessel of the same name lost during the war (see page 39). She is seen here shortly after launch, under tow to the fitting-out berths. The ship had a gross tonnage of 28,396 and was 708.7ft.long, with a speed of 22.5 knots. Six geared turbines were built by Vickers. The ship carried 631 first class and 734 tourist class passengers and her maiden voyage, to Australia, started on December 14 1948, reaching Melbourne in 26 days — ten days less than the pre-war schedule. In 1964 *Orcades* was converted into a one-class ship for 1,635 passengers, to reflect changing patterns of business, and was eventually scrapped in 1973.

Above: The second liner built for the Orient Line in the post-war years, *Oronsay* was the second vessel of the Orient fleet to carry this name, and is pictured here being launched on June 30 1950. She was a development of the *Orcades* of 1948 (above) and was 708ft long with a draught of 31ft. and a gross tonnage of 27,632. The ship was noteworthy during construction, as prefabrication and welding were used to a much greater extent than in past — Barrow once again leading the way. *Oronsay* was also fitted with Denny-Brown stabilisers which considerably checked 'roll' in heavy seas. These took the form of retractable fins, mounted beneath the waterline.

Above: *Oronsay* captured the headlines in a big way on Saturday October 28 1950 when a major fire broke out aboard the ship. More than 120 firemen from 25 brigades fought the blaze, which burned from 9pm on the Saturday evening until the early hours of Monday morning. It was ascertained that the fire started in cork and bitumen insulation in No. 2 hold, following earlier welding operations in the same area. At the height of the blaze firemen and equipment were being used from Barrow Shipyard, Barrow Borough, Dalton, Ulverston, Coniston, Grange, Carnforth, Morecambe, Lancaster, Garstang, Millom, Kendal, Milnthorpe, Workington, Whitehaven, Blackpool, Preston, Kirkby Lonsdale, Hornby, Bolton-le-Sands, Windermere and Staveley. Barrow harbour tugs *Furness* and *Ramsden* are pictured here spraying water onto the starboard hull plates, near the seat of the fire, to keep them cool and prevent buckling and rupture. No. 3 hold was flooded to prevent the fire spreading and 25 jets poured hundreds of tons of water into the blazing No. 2 hold, the extra weight of water causing *Oronsay* to develop a heavy list to port. By 4.30am on Sunday morning she was listing about 18 degrees, causing loose girderwork and equipment to crash across the decks as an extra hazard for firemen. At 6.30am the list had increased to 22 degrees, causing *Oronsay* to lean against the 150-ton crane, as shown above, and two lifeboats fell from their davits on to the dockside, prompting the hasty removal of fire fighting equipment to a safer location. The water level in Buccleuch Dock was therefore lowered to allow *Oronsay* to sit on the bottom and a hole was cut in her hull to allow water to drain out, whilst engineers flooded the starboard tanks to try and correct the list. The blaze was under control by Sunday evening, and completely extinguished, after 32 hours, on Monday morning. Two firemen were affected by smoke and fumes and a further 18 were treated in local hospitals for minor injuries. It was the worst fire at Barrow since the liner *Empress of Russia* blazed at the same berth in 1945.

Above, right: The fire aboard *Oronsay* delayed completion, and trials did not take place until 1951, prior to delivery in May 1951. She was built at a cost of £4 million and accommodated 612 first class and 804 tourist class passengers. Like her half-sister *Orcades*, she was powered by six geared steam turbines, driving twin shafts, giving a top speed of 22.5 knots. She left Tilbury on her maiden voyage to Australia on May 16 1951 arriving in Fremantle in 24 days and Melbourne in 29 days. The ship is seen here being turned through 90 degrees in Ramsden Dock, after being towed stern-first through the lifting Buccleuch Dock bridge, ready for towing out into Walney Channel.

Above: A scene of great interest in Buccleuch Dock, viewed from the road bridge, in early 1954 as a pair of tugs assist in manoeuvring *Orsova* into the centre of a very busy dock. Launched on May 14 1953 for the Orient Line and completed in March 1954, *Orsova* had a gross tonnage of 28,790 and was 722.9ft. long with a draught of 31ft. She could carry 1,480 passengers in two classes and the difference between *Orsova* and her fleet mates *Orcades* and *Oronsay* were mainly superficial. *Orsova* was the Orient Line's first, 'mastless' steamer and her extra 14ft. in length gave her stem a more pronounced rake, in comparison with her contemporaries. A new development, which was not attractive to all observers, was the stubby black stovepipe protruding from the funnel: this was designed to prevent soot and smuts landing on the upper deck. Known as 'the witches hat,' this fitting was subsequently adopted on both *Orcades* and *Oronsay*. *Orsova* was used for her company's inaugural 'round the world' sailing, arriving in London from Vancouver and Panama on July 13 1955. On the left, a cluster of warships share moorings with two of the black-liveried Isle of Man Steam Packet Company's vessels, whilst on the right is the RN aircraft carrier *HMS Majestic*, behind which, and just visible between the *Majestic* and the two cranes, is the 'carrier' *HMS Hermes*.

Below: One of the most affectionately-remembered ships built at Barrow since the last war — the Orient Line's elegant *Oriana*, laid down on September 18 1957, launched on November 3 1959 by HRH Princess Alexandra, and completed in December 1960. *Oriana* was then the biggest ship yet built in England, and one of the last of the great ocean liners. She had a gross tonnage of 41,923, an overall length of 804ft, a beam of 97.2ft. and a draught of 32ft. Extensive use of aluminium in the superstructure kept weight down and enabled the ship to have 11 decks instead of 10 and the basic foundation of her design was that she should be able to carry as many passengers, either to Australia or across the Pacific, as two of her immediate predeccessors. She required a crew of 900 and could carry 638 first, and 1496 tourist-class passengers. Built with the Australia service in mind, she was also intended for cruising and cost £14 million to construct — half as much again as the entire Orient Line fleet of 1939: She was powered by six Vickers geared turbines which gave a trials speed of 30.64 knots, and a service speed of 27.5 knots — no mean speed for a ship of such large size. Her speed and capacity would have enabled *Oriana* to deputise for Cunard's *Queen Elizabeth* on the North Atlantic service, and indeed her size meant she had to work from Southampton, instead of London. Her maiden voyage to Australia and San Francisco started on December 3 1960, just 3¼ years after her keel had been laid. *Oriana* was the first ship to be fitted with sideways propulsion, and her four manoeuvring propellers meant that her Master could handle the massive ship with relative ease in restricted waters. As this book was being prepared it was announced by her owners that she would cease operations in March of 1986, after spending recent years as an Australian cruise ship. She has since been bought by a Japanese concern, for use as a tourist attraction in Beppu Bay, South Japan. *Oriana* will be operated by the Royal Ocean Tourist Enterprise Company as a base for exhibitions, conferences and cultural activities.

THE PENINSULAR & ORIENT STEAM NAVIGATION CO.

Left: Ordered in 1930 and launched in 1931, the P&O liner *Strathnaver* (and sister ship *Strathaird*, launched the same year) did much to encourage further orders from other shipping companies, and represented the starting point for a lengthy working relationship between Vickers and P&O. *Strathnaver* (seen here being prepared to leave Barrow following completion in September 1931) and *Strathaird*, were the first ships of the P&O fleet not to appear in the company's traditional livery of black funnel, buff superstructure and black hull, and the striking white livery shown here led this pair to become known as 'the white sisters.' The ships were 664ft. long, with a beam of 80.2ft. and their impression as being very large ships was reinforced by the 'trick' of being fitted with three funnels, the front and rear structures being cosmetic dummies. These were removed during a refit in 1948, to increase deck-space.

A busy scene in Buccleuch Dock as *Strathnaver* (launched February 5 1931) is moved to allow *Strathaird* (launched July 18 1931) to be moved to its fitting-out berth. Both ships attracted much press and public attention and no P&O liner represented a greater advance on its predecessors than did *Strathnaver*. It was the first of the company's vessels designed to sail to Australia via Bombay and was unusual in being equipped with turbo-electric propulsion, with Vickers-built turbines and electrical gear by British Thomson-Houston. Service speed was 20 knots, with a top speed of 21 knots if needed, and at service speed she consumed 136 tons of oil each day. During the war *Strathnaver* and *Strathaird* acted as troopships in many parts of the world, and during their 1948 refit they were modified as single-class ships for 1,252 passengers, being used for emigration traffic to Australia, with a reduced service speed of 17.5 knots. Both ships were sold for scrap to the Shun Fung Ironworks, Hong Kong, *Strathaird* arriving at the breakers yard in summer 1961, *Strathnaver* following her sister in April 1962. The scrap value of both ships was just over £700,000.

Above: The final preparations for launch were being made when this picture of the hull of *Strathaird* was taken in July 1931, from Walney Channel. The proportions of the huge hull are clearly apparent in this picture, and one wonders that there would be sufficient depth of water to float the ship, even when the tide was in!

Left: The well-greased slipway gleams as P&O's *Strathaird* is launched on July 18 1931, with a small group of shipyard workers watching their ship enter the water for the first time. This picture shows how the drag chains were carefully arranged on each side of the slipway.

Right: Using assorted piles of timber as grandstands, the usual crowd of well-wishers watch as the white hull of the P&O liner *Strathmore* is launched into the Walney Channel on April 4 1935. The ship was sent down the slipway by the Duchess of York (now HM Queen Elizabeth, the Queen Mother) and the ceremony took place in the midst of great concern about future work at the yard. The dole queue loomed large at this time. *Strathmore*, P&O's biggest — and planned to be their fastest — liner, was launched in December 1934. She was 665ft. long overall with a beam of 82.2ft., a gross tonnage of 23,428 and was equipped with eight decks. At this time P&O had been using the 'White sisters' *Strathnaver* and *Strathaird* for just over three years and experience with these vessels led to *Strathmore's* order as a ship to improve the England-India passenger and cargo service.

Left: *Strathmore* lies at anchor, following completion in September 1935. The ship was powered by six steam turbines capable of developing 24,000 shaft horsepower giving a speed of 20.5 knots in service and she was equipped with the latest fire precautions including a comprehensive sprinkler system. All woodwork was coated in fire-resistant paint, and fireproof doors were fitted in all main corridors. *Strathmore*, which carried a crew of 510, was used in World War II as a troop transport, returning to P&O duties after 1945. In 1961 *Strathmore* was converted into a single-class ship for just over 1,000 people and she was sold in November 1963 to John S. Latsis, of Athens, who renamed her *Marianna Latsi*, for use as a hotel and pilgrim ship. She was renamed *Henrietta Latsi* in 1966, and arrived at Laspezia, Italy for breaking in May 1969, demolition commencing in September 1969.

The P&O liner *Stratheden*, launched at Barrow on June 10 1937, is fitted-out in Buccleuch Dock: in this view the ship's single funnel is being lifted on board, after fabrication as an independent unit in the Vickers workshops. The man who attached the lifting cables to the funnel can just be seen riding on top of the structure! *Stratheden*, which was completed on March 10 1938, was cruising in European waters when war broke out in September 1939 and she was requisitioned as a troop transport on March 19 1940, with sister ships *Strathmore* and *Strathallan*. Capable of carrying 530 first class and 450 tourist class passengers, *Stratheden* reopened P&O's Australian service, in 1947 and was joined on this route within two years by *Strathmore*. In the summer of 1950 *Stratheden* was chartered by Cunard for four Southampton-New York voyages, although retaining P&O colours. She was converted for single class use (1,080 berths) in November 1961 and sold to John S. Latsis in 1964, when she was renamed *Henrietta Latsi*. She switched names, becoming *Marianna Latsi* in 1966 and in 1969 she also went to Laspezia for scrap.

Right: With the murky skies of March 10 1938 made murkier still by the thick black smoke pouring from the funnels of the hard-working tugs, *Stratheden* is eased out of Ramsden Dock, through the narrow entrance lock, into the Walney Channel, where her bow will be pushed to face south, to steam away from Barrow to start work for P&O. After spending several years at Barrow, growing from the keel plates upwards, a ship like this was regarded with great affection by the townspeople in general and the men who built her in particular. A departure like this was always, and indeed still is, an emotional event. In many instances a ship would never again return to her birthplace.

Sheer elegance — the P&O liner *Himalaya* makes ready to leave Barrow following completion in August 1949. Her tugs are preparing to turn the ship as she is towed stern-first in the Ramsden Dock basin. Built as yard number 951, *Himalaya* was launched on October 5 1948 with a gross tonnage of 27,989. Designed for the Tilbury-Bombay-Australia route, *Himalaya* was 708.7ft. long, with a beam of 93.5ft. and a draught of 31ft. Powered by six steam turbines developing 42,500 shaft horsepower she achieved a maximum of 25.13 knots on trials, though normal speed was 22.5 knots: P&O was well-pleased with this performance. As built, *Himalaya* could carry 743 first class and 483 tourist class passengers. Although she was built when Vickers was in the forefront of liner design and construction, the jet airliner subsequently usurped the ship's role as a prime means of long-distance transport, and pleasure cruising became the order of the day. To reflect these changing fortunes, *Himalaya* was converted for one-class use by 1,416 passengers in 1963. *Himalaya* was sold for breaking in Taiwan in 1974, the ship arriving at Kaohsiungh on November 28 that year, with demolition starting on January 30 1975.

CUNARD WHITE STAR

Whilst the England-Australia route will always conjure memories of the Orient and P&O ships, the North Atlantic route from Liverpool and Southampton to New York will always be associated with the beautiful ships of the Cunard fleet, which had its origins with Samuel Cunard in 1839, and which is of course still active today. The Cunard Company also came to Barrow for some of its ships, and this was the scene in Ramsden Dock in 1920 as *Scythia* makes the right-angle turn, courtesy of her attendant tugs, prior to being towed into the Walney Channel. Launched on March 23 1920, *Scythia* was completed at Lorient in December 1920, after a joiners strike at Barrow stopped work. She had a gross tonnage of 19,761 and was 624ft. long, with a beam of 73.8ft. and was powered by six double-reduction geared turbines of 12,500 shaft horsepower, giving a service speed of 16 knots. *Scythia* could carry 350 first class, 350 second class and 1600 third class passengers. Her maiden voyage from Liverpool to New York started on August 20 1921, and early in her career she was involved in an accident when she collided with the White Star liner *Cedric*, off the Irish Coast. *Scythia* (and sister ships *Samaria* and *Laconia*) were built in the post-war years with a lower speed than their pre-war counterparts, partly in the mistaken belief that Trans-Atlantic speeds would be reduced in peacetime. During trooping operations in World War II she sustained damage, but was repaired and steamed more than 200,000 miles, carrying 134,000 troops before ending her military service in 1949. She returned to the North Atlantic service after a refit in 1949, and worked until withdrawal from service in the late 1950s, arriving at Inverkeithing for breaking on January 20 1958.

Right: Completed in 1905 by John Brown & Co.Ltd., Clydebank, Cunard's *Caronia* visited Barrow in 1924 for a complete refit, which included conversion from coal to oil firing of her boilers, and the fitting of supplementary lifeboats. After the refit the vessel could be recognised by the 'doubling up' of her lifeboats, hung one above the other in the davits. *Caronia* was 19,687 tons (gross) and could carry 300 first class, 350 second class and 1,100 third class passengers. She was 678ft. long with a beam of 72ft. and her two four-cylinder quadruple expansion steam engines gave a normal service speed of 18 knots. She was laid up in 1931 and sold for scrap in 1932 for £20,000 to breakers Hughes Bolckow, who subsequently sold her to Japanese breakers for £39,000.

Antonia, launched at Barrow on March 11 1921 by Sir Alfred Booth was one of a trio of similar ships, her sisters being *Ausonia* and *Andania*, both built on the Tyne, at Newcastle, in 1921 and 1922 respectively. *Antonia* (13,867 gross tonnage) was 538ft. long with a beam of 65.3ft., a draught of 27ft.and she was completed in December 1921. Her maiden voyage was from England to Canada on June 15 1922 and she carried 500 cabin-class and 1,200 third class passengers. Four boilers fed the four Vickers steam turbines of 8,500 shaft horsepower which drove twin propellers, giving the ship a speed of 15 knots. She spent the 1920s and 30s sailing between England and either Canada or the United States. *Antonia* is pictured here having been towed stern-first out of Ramsden Dock, and her bow pushed to face south by the paddle tug *Walney* on the right.

Above: The tugs have slipped their towlines and *Antonia* makes way under her own steam out of the Walney Channel. In September 1939 *Antonia* was requisitioned for war service as an Armed Merchant Cruiser, armed with four 4in., eight 21pdr. and eight 20mm (all anti-aircraft) guns. Crew complement was 596. The Admiralty bought the ship outright on March 24 1942, and converted her into a fleet repair ship, renamed as *HMS Wayland*. She served in the East Indies 1943–45 and was gutted at Cairnryan in June 1945, her hull arriving at Troon for scrap on January 22 1948. Breaking was completed by February 1949.

Launched on February 24 1925 and completed in August 1925, *Carinthia* was the second Cunard vessel to carry this name. She was originally laid down as the *Servia*, but her name was changed prior to launching. *Carinthia*, a sister ship to Cunard's *Franconia*, was 600.8ft. long, with a beam of 73.8ft a draught of 32.8ft and with a gross tonnage of 20,277. Four steam turbines of 12,500 horsepower drove twin shafts, giving the ship a speed of 17.5 knots. *Carinthia* could carry 240 first class, 460 second class and 950 third class passengers, and her maiden voyage from Liverpool to New York started on August 22 1925. In January 1940 *Carinthia* was commissioned as an Armed Merchant Cruiser, her weaponry being eight 6in. and two 3in. (anti-aircraft) guns. She was torpedoed on June 6 1940 by the German submarine U-46, off the coast of Southern Ireland, but she stayed afloat for 30 hours.

PASSENGER SHIP MISCELLANY

The *Jervis Bay*, launched at Barrow in 1922 and pictured (above) after completion, captured the hearts of the British people when in 1940 she was sunk during a valiant but suicidal defence of a merchant convoy under attack from the German pocket battleship *Admiral Scheer.* She is shown (right) being towed stern-first through the entrance to Ramsden Dock, and into Walney Channel. All Barrow-built ships had to be towed through this narrow lock — a tribute indeed to the skills of the tug skippers. Originally built for the Australian Commonwealth line of steamers with a loaded displacement of 22,500 tons, *Jervis Bay* was purchased in 1928 by Lord Kylsant's White Star Line who resold her in 1933 to the Aberdeen & Commonwealth Line. Her four steam turbines gave her a speed of 15 knots and she was just 548ft. long — a relatively small ship of no great speed, built for a specific purpose. In October 1939 she was summoned for war service and commissioned as an armed merchant cruiser, for which she was fitted with eight 6in. and two 3in. (anti-aircraft) guns, which set against the enemy's powerful naval weaponry afforded little protection. On November 5 1940, whilst *Jervis Bay* was acting as escort for an Atlantic convoy South of Iceland, the *Scheer* arrived on the scene in clear conditions, in calm water and with the convoy of 39 merchant vessels presenting ideal targets — defended only by the *Jervis Bay's* inadequate guns. However, in an act of valour for which he was posthumously awarded the Victoria Cross, Captain Fogarty Fegen turned the *Jervis Bay's* bows towards the *Scheer*, closing at his full 15 knots, ready to open fire with his small battery. Before he was even within firing range, the *Scheer's* massive long range guns were hitting the *Jervis Bay*, but her 6in. and 3in. guns were still crackling their defiance as the ship sank. It was a valiant act by the captain and crew, and other decorations for bravery were made. The *Jervis Bay* was lost, but her courage allowed 32 of the 38 ships in her care to escape. Unhindered, the *Scheer* would undoubtedly have sunk the entire convoy. One of the 32 ships which escaped, the *Sturgholm*, returned to the scene of the action after dark and rescued 65 *Jervis Bay* survivors, from life rafts and a lifeboat.

Left: With the Red Ensign fluttering on the stern, the passenger-cargo ship *Newfoundland*, launched on January 24 1925, steams south down the Walney Channel, away from Barrow. *Newfoundland* was 423.7 ft. long and was driven by quadruple-expansion four-cylinder steam engines, built by Vickers, driving twin shafts and giving the ship a speed of 15 knots. She could carry 105 cabin-class and 80 third-class passengers, and was built for the Warren Line (Liverpool) Ltd., her maiden voyage being from Liverpool to Canada and the United States. In 1935 her owners became Johnston Warren Lines Ltd and in September 1941 she became a hospital ship. *Newfoundland* was sunk by German aircraft off Salerno on September 13 1943.

Above: On a sunny day in October 1927, the Singapore-based Straits Steamship Company's *Kedah* blackens the skies over Walney Island as she leaves Barrow following completion by Vickers earlier in the month. Launched on July 16 1927, the 2,499 tons gross ship was designed to act as a feeder passenger ship for the Blue Funnel Line. She was 330ft. long with a 16ft. draught and was capable of a speed of 19 knots, driven by four geared steam turbines, built at Barrow. From 1939–43 she was an auxiliary patrol vessel, then she acted as an accommodation ship until 1946. In that year she was bought by the Kedem Israel Line Ltd and registered at Haifa, being renamed *Kedmah*, meaning 'Eastward.' She carried 260 passengers and was the first ship to raise the Israeli flag. In 1952 she was sold to her former managers Harris & Dixon Ltd and renamed *Golden Isles*, being reconditioned at Genoa, where she was subsequently laid up from June 1955 until October 1956, after which she was scrapped at Newport, Monmouthshire, by John Cashmore Ltd.

A pleasing view of the Bibby Line's *Dorsetshire*, which was converted and refitted as a troopship at Vickers yard in 1927. Between the wars the British Government had decided that its peacetime trooping requirements must be improved and started contracting with shipping companies for the provision of regular transport. Several companies, including Bibby Line, the British India Line and the P&O Steam Navigation Company found the terms attractive and Bibby converted its motor freighters *Dorsetshire* and *Somersetshire* into troopships. *Dorsetshire* was originally built by Harland & Wolff, of Belfast, in 1920 with a gross tonnage of 7,450. The ship was scrapped in 1950.

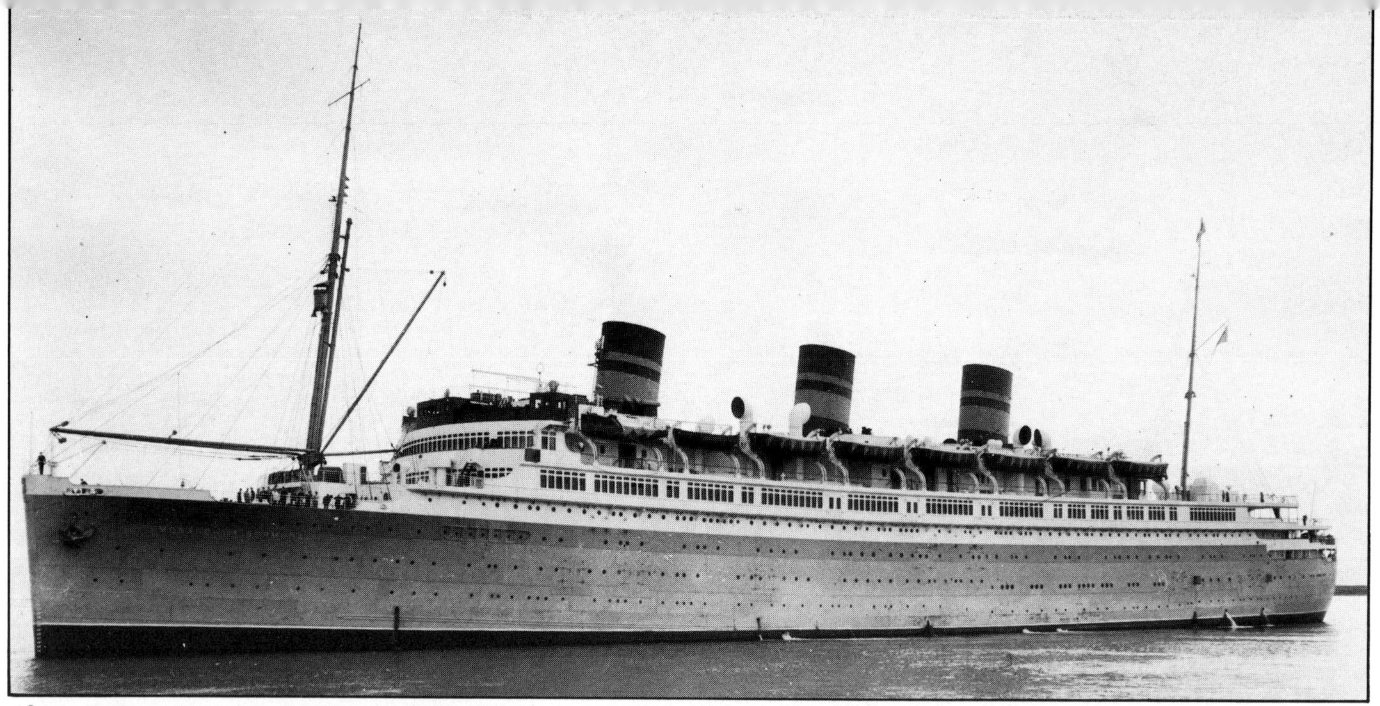

Above: Built at Newcastle for Furness Withy Ltd, the grey-hulled *Monarch of Bermuda* steams down the Walney Channel, leaving Barrow after completion at Vickers yard. Designed for service on the 'millionaires traffic' between New York and Bermuda, and operated by Furness Withy's Bermuda & West Indies Steamship Company Ltd this ship, and her consort *Queen of Bermuda* (illustrated opposite) were very luxuriously appointed. In 1930 Vickers-Armstrong's tender for building 'Monarch' had been accepted and the ship was laid down in the Walker yard at Newcastle, which was short of work and under threat of closure. Barrow was allocated the job of fitting the ship's turbo-electric propulsion machinery. She accommodated 831 first-class passengers, although a few cabins could be converted for second-class use, if required. (see also page 63).

Below: Launched on April 16 1931 and completed on August 5 1931, the *Rangatira* was built as a passenger-cargo ship for New Zealand's Union Steam Ship Company, and is seen here under tow in the Walney Channel. The ship (gross tonnage 6,152) was built for inter-island service in New Zealand and not only was she extremely popular with New Zealanders in her many years of service, but in many ways she was a 'state of the art' vessel, for her time. *Rangatira* was ordered by the USS Company to service the expanding trade between Wellington and Lyttelton: she could steam at 22 knots, carrying 716 passengers and 64 cars (36 on deck, 28 in her holds). The ship was designed for a crew of 110 and she was driven by turbo-electric machinery similar to that installed on the P&O liners *Strathnaver* and *Strathaird*. Four high-pressure oil-fired boilers supplied steam to two Vickers turbines driving generators which powered electric motors of 13,000 horsepower. She started service in New Zealand on November 3 1931 and worked until December 1965: she was subsequently sold for scrap, being towed to a Hong Kong ship breakers on November 27 1967 by the Japanese tug *Fuji Maru*. Scrapping was completed in 1968.

Left: In sunny conditions, the 22,575–tons (gross) liner *Queen of Bermuda*, sister ship to Company's *Monarch of Bermuda* (see page 52), is prepared for her launch ceremony, which took place on September 2 1932. She was built to the same design as 'Monarch', was 579ft. long, with a beam of 76.7ft. and with the accent heavily on comfort she accommodated slightly fewer passengers than her sister ship, having first-class facilities for 730 people. Eight water-tube boilers provided steam for a pair of steam turbines provided by Fraser & Chalmers, of Erith, connected to electrical equipment built by GEC, of Birmingham. A rating of 19,300 shaft horsepower gave the 'Queen' a speed of 19.25 knots, driven by four shafts. The ships both operated on the New York-Bermuda service and they became household names in the United States, where their high standard of finish and excellent quality of service were much respected. On October 28 1939 *Queen of Bermuda* was commissioned as an Armed Merchant Cruiser, fitted with seven 6in. and two 3in. (anti-aircraft) guns, together with a single aircraft. She became a troopship in 1943, returning to her old service after the war. In 1961 she was extensively refitted by Harland & Wolff at Belfast, from where she emerged with a single large funnel and new boilers. Her last new New York-Bermuda-New York cruise was in 1966, after which she was sold for scrap, arriving at Faslane complete with all fixtures and fittings. As scrap she was worth £250.000.

Shortly before delivery to her owner, *Queen of Bermuda* is pictured undergoing speed trials on the measured mile on the River Clyde, in 1933. The 'Queen' and 'Monarch' were much 'squatter' in profile than contemporary liners of other companies, the reason for this being that the entrance to Hamilton harbour, Bermuda, was surrounded by coral reefs, the navigation of which required the ships to have minimum length and draught consistent with their size, resulting in a congested appearance amidships. Nevertheless the ships were much loved by Bermudians, who turned out in force to bid farewell to the 'Queen' when she sailed from Bermuda for the last time.

Right: Incredible though it might seem at a first glance, this four-masted barque was built by Vickers in 1933, the same year that *Queen of Bermuda* was completed! The *Almirante Saldanha*, seen here being towed through Buccleuch Dock's lifting railway bridge, was built for the Brazilian Navy as a sail training ship, and was 307.3ft. long with a beam of 52ft. and a mean draught of 18.3ft. She was launched on December 19 1933 and had a fully loaded displacement of 3,825 tons. *Almirante Saldanha* was equipped to accommodate about 300 seamen, 34 warrant officers, 100 cadets and 25 officers — a total complement of 459. The elegant ship was capable of carrying 25,990 square feet of sail and was designed to train young officers and seamen in traditional techniques, but she was fitted nevertheless with an auxiliary six-cylinder 1,400 horse-power diesel engine, which gave her an endurance of 12,000 miles at 11 knots. An interesting aspect of the design of the ship's electrical equipment was that it had to function well when inclined at 15 degrees in any direction, as these conditions would apply when the vessel was under sail and heeling in the wind. All bearings therefore required special attention and construction. Weaponry fitted to the *Almirante Saldanha* included four 4in., one 3in. (anti-aircraft), one 13mm (anti-aircraft) and four 3pdr. guns, together with two machine guns and a single 21in. diameter torpedo tube. She cost £314,000 to construct. In the late 1950s she became an oceanographic survey ship and was completely rebuilt and dismasted in 1964; the *Almirante Saldanha* was still in service at the time of going to press, though she bears little resemblance to the elegant sailing vessel shown here.

The unusual sight of a 'mini-liner' in 'assembly kit' form, aboard a train at Barrow in Furness! The vessel is the 251-ton motor vessel *Teal*, built for the London Midland & Scottish Railway's Lake Windermere pleasure service, in 1936. Although 10 miles long, Windermere is land-locked and the LMS turned to Vickers-Armstrong when it required new vessels in the middle 1930s. The plan adopted was that the ship was built at Barrow in the traditional fashion, each part given a code number, and then dismantled for transhipment piecemeal, by rail, to Lakeside — a distance of about 15 miles.

Left: Having successfully been transported by rail from Barrow to Lakeside *Teal* was rebuilt on the Lakeside slipway, according to the numbered parts, after which the vessel was launched into Windermere, where she is still in service today, in modified form. *Teal* is pictured here at her official launch on July 4 1936, with well wishers standing on the temporary railway siding on which she arrived at Lakeside. This slipway is still used each winter when *Teal*, *Swan* and *Tern* are winched out of the water for repainting. *Swift*, fourth member of the lake fleet, is now out of service, and converted into a floating museum presently housing the 'Campbell Legend' exhibition.

Teal might have been a small ship by Vickers-Armstrong's normal standards but she was elegant and well-designed for her role on Windermere, and she is pictured here at Lakeside, shortly after the launch, shown above. *Teal* was 135ft. long with a beam of 25ft, driven by a pair of 16-cylinder Gleniffer diesel engines of 320 brake horsepower giving a service speed of 11 knots. As built, *Teal* (and sister ship *Swan*, built and launched in the same way in 1938) carried 800 passengers in two classes on three decks. *Teal's* open bridge afforded little protection for her skipper and quartermaster, who worked long hours in Lakeland's variable weather. Covered bridges were not provided until much later and subsequent alterations converted *Teal* and *Swan* into single-class ships, and added refreshment facilities. *Teal* is still at work today, under Master James Jackson, whose father was the *Teal's* skipper earlier in her career.

Above: A passenger-cargo ship of 13,482 tons (gross) the *Awatea* was launched on February 25 1936 for New Zealand's Union Steam Ship Company, for which Vickers had built the smaller *Rangatira* in 1931, (see page 52). Built for the New Zealand-Australia route, *Awatea's* name was the Maori for 'Eye of the Dawn' and she was a beautiful ship of very elegant proportions. She was 527.3ft. long with a beam of 74.2ft, powered by six Vickers-built steam turbines of 22,500 shaft horsepower, giving a speed of 22.5 knots. Following trials on the River Clyde's measured mile, *Awatea* sailed for New Zealand on August 5 1936, reaching Wellington via the Panama Canal in 28 days, after which she commenced her express service across the Tasman Sea on September 15. She was taken over for war service in September 1939 and on November 11 1942 was engaged in operations in the Mediterranean when she was bombed by the Luftwaffe, off Bougie breakwater, Algeria. Under attack from six bombers, *Awatea's* anti-aircraft guns put up a stout defence, but exploding bombs caused severe damage and started a fire and eventually the order was given to abandon ship. She sank the following day. By 1942 *Awatea* had logged 576,132 miles in service in her short life of six years, transporting during her wartime service 3,600 New Zealand and Australian airmen to Canada, 17,500 troops to various battle zones, including North Africa, as well as 900 repatriated civilians.

With the launch ceremonies completed, the Argentine Government's passenger-cargo ship *Eva Peron* is prepared by tugs for the short trip to her fitting-out berth on August 25 1949. This modern-looking ship was completed in April 1950, with a gross tonnage of 12,627 and an overall length of 530ft. Capable on trials of a speed of 19.7 knots, *Eva Peron* was built to a similar design to the *Presidente Peron*, built by Vickers for Argentina, launched on November 3 1948 and completed in July 1949. Both ships were driven by four Vickers-built geared turbines and twin propeller shafts, giving a service speed of 18.5 knots. Accommodation was provided for 96 first class passengers. In 1955 *Eva Peron* was renamed *Uruguay* and *Presidente Peron* became *Argentina*, her owners being then recorded as Empresa Lineas Maritimas Argentinas, the Government's State Merchant Fleet.

DELIVERING THE GOODS

ALTHOUGH the impressive passenger liners invariably captured much publicity, because of their glamorous image and evocative names, Vickers also built many cargo ships of various sizes which earned their living, out of the public eye, carrying a wide variety of merchandise. The cargo vessels, which sometimes had limited passenger facilities, might have been less glamorous than the great ocean liners, but they represented important work for the ship builders of Barrow and any pictorial examination of this area would be incomplete without at least a brief look at these ships.

Below: Launched at Barrow on September 14 1920 for the Donaldson Line, the *Cortona* was completed in March 1921. She was 414.ft. long with a beam of 55.7 ft. and a gross tonnage of 7,093. Four boilers provided steam for two Vickers-built turbines which drove a single shaft, giving *Cortona* a speed of 12 knots. She was torpedoed and sunk on July 11 1942.

Above: Also built for the Glasgow-based Donaldson Line, the *Moveria* was launched on October 10 1924 as a passenger-cargo ship and completed in January 1925. She was 398.3ft. long and driven by an eight-cylinder oil engine, built by Vickers, of 2,700 brake horsepower, which gave a speed of 11.5 knots.

Left: The Centuary Coal Company's *Collier No. 1*, immediately after launch into the Walney Channel on May 6 1924. The 1,858 tons (gross) collier was rapidly completed and was ready for delivery within a month, fitted with Vickers-built compound two-cylinder steam engines with a shaft horsepower rating of 850, giving a service speed of 9.5 knots.

Right: The *Geraldine Mary*, a wood pulp and timber carrier launched at Barrow on August 19 1924, was built for the Anglo-Newfoundland Shipping Company Ltd. The ship was 422ft. long, with a gross tonnage of 7,244 and capable of 11 knots, driven by 3,000 shaft horsepower steam engines. *Geraldine Mary* was torpedoed and sunk on August 4 1940.

Left: The oil tanker *British Adventure*, built for the BP Tanker Company Ltd, London, is launched on December 12 1950. Completed in September 1951, the ship was of 18,492 tons (gross) and had a dead weight capacity of 28,726 tons, with an overall length of 643ft. and a draught of 34ft. Two geared turbines built by Vickers drove a single propeller shaft. The ship was eventually sold to Greek owners. This was the first 'tanker' built by Vickers in the post-war years and by, 1965 a further 18 oil-carrying ships, of steadily increasing size, had been built at Barrow.

Capable of carrying more than 100,000 tons of oil *British Admiral* was the biggest tanker in Britain at the time of its construction. Seen here under tow in the Walney Channel, *British Admiral* was ordered by the BP Tanker Company Ltd in December 1961, laid down on December 3 1962 and launched by HRH Queen Elizabeth II on March 17 1965. The ship was Europe's first 100,000-tonner and the launch date had to be chosen very carefully with a suitably high tide. It wouldn't be regarded as particularly big today, but 'Admiral's' length of 917.5ft. and 128ft. beam seemed massive indeed in 1965. The ship was launched with all its machinery already installed, contrary to normal practice, and was fitted with its own television camera on the foremast, for navigational purposes. *British Admiral* carried in excess of 103,000 tons of oil in ten wing tanks and seven centre tanks, and could travel at 15.5 knots, powered by turbines of 25,000 shaft horsepower. At its peak, work on *British Admiral* occupied 1,440 staff.

SHIPPING activity around Barrow was of course dominated by shipbuilding and repair in the Vickers yard, but the town also hosted shipbreaking operations by T.W. Ward & Co.Ltd, and there were commercial cargoes being moved though the docks as a port. This further enriched the already diverse pattern of maritime business and this section of the book is a 'pot pourri' of general scenes around Barrow's docks, and in the Walney Channel. It will give an idea of the vessels which could be seen at Barrow in the years when the Sankey Collection of photographs was growing. Many pictures were simple, everyday scenes of no special interest whatsoever at the time, and there were doubtless those observers who looked in disbelief as my father and I busied ourselves with our cameras around the docks. The passing of the years has rendered these everyday scenes of very special interest indeed.

Left: Sailing down the Walney Channel is Barrow pilot boat No. B2 *Albacore*, which had originally been built at Fleetwood as a fishing smack in 1880, and later converted for use by pilots. It was 64ft. long with a beam of 16ft. and it survived until 1924, when it was broken up at Roa Island.

AROUND THE DOCKS

An evocative scene in Devonshire Dock, now the site of the massive new submarine building facility which dominates the skyline from many parts of Barrow, as the tugs *Cartmel* (at the bow) and *Furness* guide the Swedish barque *Favell* (registered at Helsingford) towards the grain shed, with the floating dock in the right background, and one of the Isle of Man Steam Packet Company's ships on the left.

Right: The barque *Whinlatter*, moored in the docks alongside the convict ship *Success.* Both ships were probably at Barrow for scrapping at Ward's yard.

Left: With smoke billowing from her short funnel, her pumps working and all three masts damaged, the sailing ship *Kelburn* presents a rather sorry face to the world in Barrow docks. Built in 1899 at Glasgow, the 308ft long vessel had a gross tonnage of 2,579. In August 1910 *Kelburn* had been stranded in Morecambe Bay, and she was probably due for scrapping here.

Right: Prior to the opening of the lifting bridge over the Walney Channel in 1908, all traffic between the town and Walney Island was carried by this steam-powered ferry, built at Barrow for the Furness Railway Company. It was launched on March 15 1902 and was 72ft long, 38ft wide and had a draught of 4ft 6in. The ferry was coal-fired and dragged itself across the Channel by means of two chains. The opening of the bridge made the ferry redundant, and it was subsequently transferred to Southampton.

Left, above: Berthed alongside the grain store in Devonshire Dock, opposite the fitting-out berths, is the *Chiverstone*, a steam ship built in 1897 at Thornaby on Tees. The ship was 330ft. long, had a beam of 43.1ft. and a gross tonnage of 2,946.

Left, below: The steamship *Monkseaton*, built at Wallsend, on the Tyne, in 1883, is berthed in Ramsden Dock. Owned by Thompson Dunfield of Newcastle upon Tyne, the ship was 2,772 tons (gross) and was 325.6ft. long with a beam of 39.7ft.

Below: Flying the 'stars and stripes' from its foremast, the oil tanker *Delaware* is berthed in Ramsden Dock. This ship was built in 1893 for the Anglo-American Oil Company Ltd, was 345ft. long and had a gross tonnage of 3,855. One of the Furness Railway's 0-6-0 tender engines is just visible in the distance to the right of the ship.

Above: A typical working day in Ramsden Dock. A uniformed officer on the upper deck of the steam ship *Quernmore* keeps a watchful eye on me as I photograph his ship being towed stern-first through the dock. A couple of men in a rowing boat are hauling out a second towline from the stern of *Quernmore*, which was owned by Furness Withy & Co.Ltd. On the left is the *Bogan*, a turret-decker ship built by Doxford as the *Orangemoor* in 1911 for the Moor Line. She was torpedoed and sunk by a German submarine in 1941, en-route from Gourock to Durban.

Right: Raising steam in Ramsden Dock on May 6 1924 is the Furness Withy steam ship *Dromore*, a 6,398 tons (gross) vessel built in Stockton-on-Tees in 1913. The ship was employed on Furness Withy's Barrow-New York service.

For the last picture in this book I have returned to the ocean liner, for it is this beautiful breed which strikes a chord with many people, and which prompts many happy memories for me. *Monarch of Bermuda* was built at Newcastle, but was brought to Barrow for the installation of its Vickers – built turbo-electric machinery, and the 22,000 tons (gross) ship is seen here being eased through the narrow entrance to Ramsden Dock, with the steam tugs *Cartmel* (left) and *Wrestler* at her bow. The golden age of the liner has now gone and it is highly unlikely that Vickers will ever again build ships of this kind, but the company remains at the forefront of design and innovations, in submarine building for the Royal Navy, thus maintaining a very proud tradition. Long may it continue!

BIBLIOGRAPHY

THE FOLLOWING sources were used as reference material in the preparation of this book:
West Coast Steamers .... C.L. Duckworth & G.E. Langmuir.
Railway and Other steamers .... C.L. Duckworth & G.E. Langmuir.
British Passengers Liners of the Five Oceans .... Cmdr. C.R. Vernon Gibbs RN.
Historic Cunard Liners .... Philip Rentell.
A Century of Shipbuilding .... Tom Clark.
British Battleships: A History of Design, Construction & Armament .... Oscar Parkes.
Conways All the World's Fighting Ships 1860–1905.
A Century of Naval Construction .... D.K. Brown.
Battleships and Battle Cruisers 1905–1907 .... Siegried Breyer.
British Vessels Lost at Sea .... HMSO.
Warships in Profile Volume 1 .... John Wingate DSC.
The Metal Fighting Ship .... E.H.H. Archibald.
The Encyclopedia of the World's Warships .... Hugh Lyon.
The Observers Directory of Royal Naval Submarines .... M.P. Cocker.
The Official Vickers Yardlist 1873–1963,.
Various volumes: Jane's Fighting Ships, Lloyds Register of Shipping.

Publisher's Acknowledgement

Silver Link Publishing would like to add its thanks and gratitude to David Hughes, Curator of Barrow Museum, for much valued help and advice given in the production of this book. Special thanks are also due to Cumbria County Library, Barrow in Furness, and to Michael Crowdy, John Pryce and Kevin O'Donoghue, of the World Ship Society, and to Michael Walker, of Morecambe. Their assistance and guidance was much appreciated.

Silver Link Publishing Ltd